LIFE WORLD LIBRARY

GREECE

OTHER BOOKS BY THE EDITORS OF LIFE

LIFE Nature Library

LIFE Pictorial Atlas of the World
    with The Editors of Rand McNally

The Epic of Man

The Wonders of Life on Earth
    with Lincoln Barnett

The World We Live In
    with Lincoln Barnett

The World's Great Religions

LIFE's Picture History of Western Man

The LIFE Treasury of American Folklore

America's Arts and Skills

The Second World War
    with Winston S. Churchill

LIFE's Picture History of World War II

Picture Cook Book

LIFE Guide to Paris

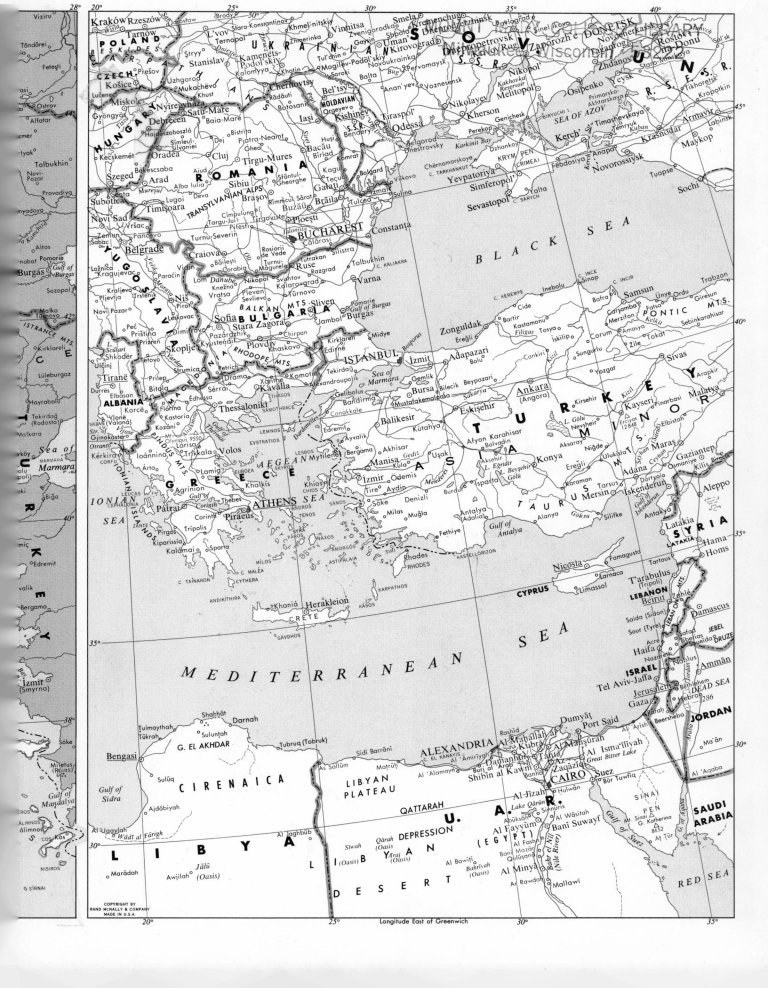

LIFE WORLD LIBRARY

GREECE

by Alexander Eliot

and The Editors of LIFE

A
STONEHENGE
BOOK
TIME INCORPORATED   NEW YORK

COVER: The sparkling belfries
of a church on Skyros,
a Greek island in the Aegean Sea,
rise above the pleasing patchwork
of the village roofs.

ABOUT THE WRITER

Alexander Eliot, author of the interpretive text for this volume in the LIFE World Library, is an experienced journalist who now lives in Greece. Art Editor of TIME Magazine for 15 years, Mr. Eliot resigned from Time Inc. in 1960 to accept a Guggenheim Fellowship for study of Greece and the Middle East as "spiritual homelands of the western world." He has since resided near Athens. His books include *Proud Youth,* a novel; *Three Hundred Years of American Painting,* an art history; *Sight and Insight,* a discussion of his own art philosophy; and *Earth, Air, Fire and Water,* a discourse on his personal view of life.

EL4

Contents

TIME INC. BOOK DIVISION

EDITOR
Norman P. Ross

COPY DIRECTOR   ART DIRECTOR
William Jay Gold   *Edward A. Hamilton*

CHIEF OF RESEARCH
Beatrice T. Dobie

EDITORIAL STAFF FOR "GREECE"

EDITOR, LIFE WORLD LIBRARY	*Oliver E. Allen*
ASSISTANT TO THE EDITOR	*David S. Thomson*
DESIGNER	*Ben Schultz*
CHIEF RESEARCHER	*Grace Brynolson*
RESEARCHERS	*Barbara Ballantine, Edward Brash,*
	Louise Samuels, Helen R. Turvey,
	Ava Weekes, Edmund White, Linda Wolfe
PICTURE RESEARCHERS	*Margaret K. Goldsmith,*
	Mary Elizabeth Davidson, Sue Bond
ART ASSOCIATE	*Robert L. Young*
ART ASSISTANTS	*James D. Smith, William Gedney*
COPY STAFF	*Marian Gordon Goldman,*
	Carol Henderson, Dolores A. Littles
PUBLISHER	*Jerome S. Hardy*
GENERAL MANAGER	*John A. Watters*

LIFE MAGAZINE

EDITOR   MANAGING EDITOR   PUBLISHER
Edward K. Thompson   *George P. Hunt*   *C. D. Jackson*

The text for the chapters of this book was written by Alexander Eliot, for the picture essays by Jay Brennan and David S. Thomson. Valuable help in the preparation of the book was provided by the following members of Time Inc.: James Burke and Dmitri Kessel, LIFE staff photographers; Richard Meek, Time Inc. contributing photographer; Doris O'Neil, Chief, LIFE Picture Library; Donald Bermingham, TIME-LIFE News Service; and Content Peckham, Chief, Bureau of Editorial Reference.

Introduction

Modern Greece was shaped on the anvil of war. Whereas in western Europe the guns of World War II were silenced in 1945, the Greek people were condemned to struggle with the Communist invaders for four grinding years thereafter —often village against village and sometimes brother against brother—before they could vindicate the right of 20th Century Greece to stand with the free world, which inherited freedom from Athens 2,500 years ago.

Nor was this modern issue of freedom a foregone conclusion. Stalin coveted Greece. It would have been a rich prize for communism to add to the satellites on Russia's borders, and Moscow schemed to win it. Had it not been for the assistance to the Greek people, first of Great Britain and then of the United States, today a Communist colony might well posture malevolently athwart the Aegean crossroads.

It was not until August of 1949 that the last armed Communist was driven by Marshal Papagos and General Van Fleet from the slopes of Mount Grammos into the dubious sanctuary of Albania. Exhausted though Greece was, it promptly showed its appreciation of western aid by contributing troops to fight with the United Nations Command in Korea. In 1952, Greece joined the North Atlantic Treaty Organization as a full partner, and eight years later, when Stalin's successor threatened to pulverize the Acropolis unless Greece abandoned a NATO commitment, the answer was that although the temples on the sacred hill might indeed disappear, the ideals for which they stood were indestructible.

Thus Greece consolidated its independence.

In the pages that follow, Alexander Eliot tells how it has been with the Greeks from ancient times down to the present day, and he describes anew the impact of the Athenian mind on all the subsequent thinking of mankind. It is a fascinating story that never grows old and is never finished. Mr. Eliot tells it well, for he has an understanding eye and a poet's heart.

This too is a pictorial book. While the author emphasizes the classical heritage of Greece, the illustrations will help you to realize that notwithstanding its antiquity, Greece is the newest of the Mediterranean lands in terms of those facilities and comforts that beguile the visitor within its gates.

The reason is that when the Communist war ended, Greece was so broken that almost everything had to be rebuilt. Highways, houses and towns, power and water supply, communications facilities, sanitation, hotels and transportation—all these things are new.

So by revised count the resources of Greece are these:

The Greek people—sophisticated, ambitious, articulate, hospitable and lively—a people tempered in the flames of strife and dedicated to the ways of the western world.

Lacking many of the raw materials of industrialization, Greece nevertheless offers a supply of intelligent and adaptable workers. It invites foreign capital into an environment of stable government, which is enacting economic legislation geared to Greece's membership in the European Common Market.

And to the surpassingly lovely geography of Greece and its cultural heritage, the country can now offer visitors the modern amenities that render hospitality memorable.

Whether you travel or not, this book will bring you closer to the Acropolis.

ELLIS O. BRIGGS
former U.S. Ambassador to Greece

Tourists are dwarfed by the massive columns of the Propylaea, the gateway to Athens' Acropolis which stands on the western front of the

8

hill. *The columns were spaced widely enough to admit chariots.*

1

The Clear Land

AN immortal tale tells of a "Clear Land" where colors are purer and the forms of things are finer than on earth. At first the Clear Land seems only a radiant reflection of earthbound countries. The trees, houses and mountains known to everyday experience are all outlined there with dazzling clarity upon the shining air. "Then comes the strange part. When you are perfectly at home there you see again that it is very like our lower world!" Such conditions seem to come true in Greece. Even the Greek battle cry has unlooked-for resonance. *Aera!* the fighting men sing out, meaning "Air!" Greece is a Clear Land, where the sun caresses the mountains and where life itself has a clearer shape. It does not seem surprising that Greece was the setting, some 2,500 years ago, for one of man's best efforts to define the nature and purposes of life on earth.

Awakening in this Clear Land is often an especially keen delight. The roosters which are everywhere about help you to it at an early hour. With luck you may see the first pale rosy rays spiking out from behind a dark mountain. This is the hand of "rosy fingered Dawn," the same that Homer, the first and greatest of the poets of western civilization, knew so many dewy mornings ago. And once again the god Apollo's golden chariot comes winging up over the steep countryside, making the bare peaks shine like crystal above the cold violet valleys and the still, dark sea.

THE roosters crow the louder; in this country nothing quiets them. But the nightingales fall silent now, or rather their rich silver improvisations vanish like light into light. The thrilling shriek of Athena's silent-winged owl too is stilled. The owl huddles deep in a plane tree by a bubbling spring; it fears the ravens whose black-suited flocks are flapping heavily to their larcenous work in the sun-swept fields. Sarcastically the black robbers light on a breeze-teased scarecrow, a tattered coat upon a stick, while cawing up the sudden warmth of day.

The village innkeeper puts out a single table and chair, tentatively, like a tortoise thrusting out a foot. Sparrows peck and chitter on the cobblestones of the village's steep and winding street. Now they fly up like brown leaves in a gust as a peasant girl appears. She is all in black, but her smile and her glancing eyes gleam white as the morning. The innkeeper's mangy hound stretches out his forepaws and growls approval as the girl goes by. Her thick black hair is coiled in a single braid to signify maidenhood. She passes, straight and graceful, with a tall brown jug upon her head. The girl is on her way to the spring beneath the plane tree, where the owl dozes already and a serpent sleeps too beneath the roots.

What's for breakfast? Eggs, if the hens have been obliging. Otherwise *feta*, a mild crumbly cheese made from goat's milk. And fresh warm bread to go with it. Then comes the coffee, late but sweet and strong, in a tiny cup that is one third full of gooey sediment.

The word for bill is *logariasmos*—as in logarithms. But before you can ask for yours the leisurely innkeeper may disappear for a while and then return with a glass of wine. It will be piny resinated wine called *retsina*, as tangy as the morning air. The accounting may come to 15 or 20 cents. Your breakfast would have been considered a good dinner in many Greek homes. For the fact is that in this loveliest of all possible lands, under the cool breezes and strong sunshine, meat is a luxury and many of the people are thin-ribbed.

Amongst these old mountains Pan and the nymphs are dancing still, and sometimes voiceless invisible hunger also dances. Greece as a whole resembles an improbable rock garden, fragrant with herbs and wild flowers, sea-bathed on every hand, beautifully sculptured and yet harsh in its own way. Like marble it is gleaming and lovely in the distance, hard-edged close by and chill beneath the fingers. This rocky southeast corner of Europe has given more to the world perhaps than any other place. But its fruits are of the spirit.

Of course there are rich Greeks, very rich ones indeed, at Athens and a few resorts. Most famous are the great shipowners, among the wealthiest men in the world. This plutocratic circle is a society unto itself, like a fabulous island in its own greenback sea. The other eight million or more Greeks know all about this world, but not at firsthand. In the Greek countryside, millionaires appear as rarely as the vanishing gray crane, wolf and wild boar.

RURAL Greece produces its own "haves" and "have-nots," yet here the distinction between the two is slight. The "have-nots" mainly endure by dint of day labor at low pay, when they can find work at all. What the "haves" possess is likely to be a tiny, tilting tobacco field or a few scrawny olive trees or a scraggly flock of goats, or perhaps a rowboat in which to search the nighttime waters for fish, or a *taverna* with two tables and a barrel of wine, or a job on a freighter and with it the chance to leave the ship and settle in a land of opportunity, such as Australia. Greece is far from being a soft touch for the workingman.

Yet the Greek poor are gallant, gracious and unbowed. Their chief strength lies where it always has—in nature. The vast majority of the Greek people depends on nature and loves it, not in some vague, romantic manner but in actuality. Nature in their experience *is* absolutely beautiful, and also the clear source of all they have. So in general they may be said to live a hard life well.

Politics intrigue the country Greek, but he has small influence as a voter. The government, a constitutional monarchy, stands for social welfare. However, Greek political life remains largely the province of professionals, who keep returning themselves and their friends to power. Shipping, the nascent industries and the cruelly haphazard mechanism of distribution are mainly controlled by influential families. The Communist Left poses as the friend of the poor, but conspires to lead the country by the nose straight into the Russian camp. The Right and Center parties meanwhile have been accused of treating the poor as troublesome statistics—which may be on occasion be juggled.

GEOGRAPHY works against national unity. The mainland—a laterally split peninsula about 400 miles from north to south—is chiefly composed of mountains divided by narrow valleys and plains. Some 400 islands make up a fifth of the total land area. Greece consists of innumerable small communities, each cut off from the other by the hills or the sea. As a result, the many conquerors who ruled Greece from ancient times almost to the present found it virtually impossible to impose country-wide political or economic control. Even in this age of rapid communications many of the remoter regions of Greece seem quite cut off from the capital, Athens, although the country as a whole is only slightly larger than New England.

Something less than a quarter of Greece is arable, and a mere tenth (5,000 square miles) consists of good bottom land. The burning, beautiful isles provide the least nourishment: some of them survive on sailors' remittances alone. Yet there are some fruitful patches of Greek soil, exceptions to the general rule. One is the Amphissian plain below Delphi in central Greece. Millions of tough old olive trees make the plain a silver-green sea on the land.

An even more important exception is the broad plain of Thessaly, between central Greece and the large northern province of Macedonia. Here many of the prospering peasants are still "in costume," wearing embroidered brown, black, yellow, red and white, with flowing sleeves for the women and sometimes a tight bright orange bodice. At the northwestern edge of the plain hovers a towering fountain of rock, Meteora, where monasteries perch upon the pinnacles like storks' nests on chimney pots.

West of Meteora an abominable road winds up and up into an alpine country of dark skies and pointed firs: the Pindus Mountains. Not long ago the giant sheep dogs of this region revolted and made mutton of their masters. It is said that troops were needed to restore human government. The potholed road over the pass—incredibly enough the only main road between northeastern and northwestern Greece —winds down at last into the province of Epirus. Far below the winding road Lake Ioannina appears, emerald colored, with purple clouds in its depths. The town beside this still lake has immense medieval battlements, minarets left over from Turkish times and an aura of sad romance. It is like a once vivid carpet left to fade upon the shores of sleep.

EVERYWHERE in Greece one meets with history and welcome, hand in hand. South of the province of Epirus lies Aetolia, then the Gulf of Corinth, then high Arcadia, and Olympia, the site of the ancient games. At Olympia the pebbly river, towering pines, olive trees and gentle hills mantled with daisies all conspire to soothe one's soul. The Olympic Games were held here regularly for a millennium—despite wars, plagues and famines round about.

Olympia is the great shrine of peace and fair play. Yet strangely enough it was founded to commemorate a "fixed" race. Far from wishing to conceal the fact, the ancients celebrated it. Witness the huge and splendid pediment that still remains from the east gable of Olympia's Temple of Zeus. The hero of this sculpture, a prince named Pelops, was a schemer who secretly tampered with the wheel of his rival's chariot. At the first turn, off came the wheel; the chariot of course collapsed, the horses panicked and the driver was dragged to his death. Pelops, smiling, drove on to victory. Prospering mightily in the years that followed, he bequeathed his own name to the whole region south of the Gulf of Corinth, the Peloponnesus.

SOUTH of Olympia lies "Mani Country." The Maniots claim direct descent from the ancient warlike Spartans, and they may well be correct. Among this flat-bellied folk, mustachios sometimes grow eight inches or more in length. Male Maniots are welcomed into the world with gunfire salutes. The infants themselves are even referred to as "guns"—and enrolled at birth in the tribe's own immemorial blood feuds. The rugged peninsula of the Mani has never really been subdued. Down the long centuries its corsairs preyed on Phoenician, Greek, Roman, Byzantine, Venetian and Turkish shipping. Mani sea caves, crammed with treasure, have been "home" to many a rich merchant held for ransom and many a poor sailor held for sale. Fishermen's nets and gallon tins of *ouzo* (the Greek Pernod) are about all that these caves keep today. The Maniots, devotees of blood and Bacchus, have a queer hang-over cure: pressing half of a cucumber to the brow, they prance along the tops of the cliffs like unicorns.

Although Maniot families have reason to fear each other, travelers among them need not be afraid. Zeus, the classical "father of the gods," was also the "protector of strangers." To turn away from one's door or dinner table any beggar, suppliant, pilgrim or plain pagan tourist meant to risk the god's thunderbolt. It still does. Hospitality remains the rule in all remote parts of Greece. The poorest shepherd shares his bread and wine with the passerby, no matter how little of either he may have. Even a hermit in a high crevice will scare up a few berries for you from along the cliff. This gives a spiritual dimension to the Greek countryside —something which the swiftly increasing tourist facilities can only counterfeit and destroy.

Besides hospitality, the Greeks have a second distinguishing trait: they smile upon friend and foe alike. This habit can be seen even in the "archaic" smile which illuminates their earliest sculptures. In the *Iliad*, Homer describes how the Trojans trembled with terror when Ajax advanced "smiling under his threatening brows." Still today, a smile on the face of a Greek mechanic or politician is likely to spell trouble. There is an old adage of the New York underworld which runs: "Never try to rob a Greek candy store." If invited to "reach for the ceiling," the sleepy-looking proprietor smiles and prepares to defend his few dollars with his life.

Greece was always a crossroads of migrating peoples: Dorians, Goths, Franks, Turks, Serbs and many more. Its emergence as a modern nation has obscured the diversity of its people. Just a few centuries ago the scattered inhabitants were wont to pray: "From the Greeks of Athens, the Jews of Thessaloniki and the Turks of Negropont [the island of Euboea], good Lord deliver us!" With all this, Greece has kept an astonishing continuity. Like some tiny China, it civilizes its own conquerors.

THE Minoan culture of Crete, which flourished from 2400 B.C. down to 1400 B.C., inspired Homer and the Hellenic world. Classical Greek culture became in turn a powerful influence on the civilization of conquering Rome. The eastern half of the Roman Empire, especially, absorbed and then disseminated elements of Greek culture. Its outgrowth, the Christian culture of Byzantium, lives on still in Greece. Moreover, after 3,000 years, modern Greek *demotiki* is as close to Homer's own language as modern English is to Chaucer's. Most remarkable is the pervasive influence of ancient Greece on all western thought. The modern world would be far different, in everything from science to our faith in the dignity of man, had the Greeks not shown the way.

Can the nature of the Greeks be summarized? Realism, quickness and courage have always stood high among its positive aspects. The shadow sides of these three virtues are cynicism, instability and cruelty—of course. Yet to any halfway sympathetic eye, Greek character presents more lights than shadows. There is nothing misty or monstrous about the Greeks. The land itself gives them something of its own essential clarity. The shining air seems to enter the very spirits of the people. Even their "sins," as Goethe pointed out, "have light and spark."

CUSTOMARILY, visitors to Greece and writers on the subject begin at Athens and ray out from there. Such procedure is natural, yet may produce a blurred impression. The capital itself is modern and faceless except in part. It has broad avenues, a subway, shops smart and otherwise, hotels the same, plenty of neon (the old Greek word for "new") and mile upon mile of concrete office and apartment warrens. The proximity of beach and mountain makes it habitable still. A public garden and some small squares set with café tables relieve the monotony. But the relics of the past have more sense of life about them than the latest things. Compare the Parthenon, for instance, with the towering new Hilton Hotel. Both dominate the skyline: which one seems to be a hollow shell?

Or compare the swank, dull Kolonaki district with the run-down but delightful Plaka. The Plaka, comprising a few steep acres on the northern slope of the Acropolis, is a surprisingly cheerful remnant of Athens enslaved. Some of these twisting alleys and staircases leading straight into tiny houses were built under Turkish rule, when Athens was reduced to a mere village. It is a place of whitewash and rich shadows, of coffee roasting in the open, of howling cats, street fights, passion on the stairs and a profusion of flowers growing in oilcans. Moreover it can be a place of refuge from the huge blank unreality of the city below.

Visitors invariably note and appreciate Athenian courtesy. Equally obvious is the local passion for politics—as a spectator sport. Upward of 14 daily papers are on the streets, carrying all shades of opinion. In the rather Germanic House of Parliament, a onetime royal palace, the statesmen often shout and bang their desks. Outside, the populace makes fairly frequent and not always peaceful demonstrations, which are swiftly dispersed. Visitors who remain long enough to experience Athens society find it cosmopolitan, smooth, respectable. Rich and poor Athenians alike appear to be a little heavier than their country cousins—heavier in spirit. The Athens area contains roughly two million citizens, about a quarter of the national total. Yet they are not Greece.

In the course of time Athens becomes a burden on the mind. It gives rise to long, dark thoughts about economics, politics, history and the "deep, underlying problems" that remain so dear to bureaucrats and journalists alike. In Greece, as in almost every country, there are terrible inequities, failures of justice and of mercy too. Democracy struck root first of all in Greece, however, and as George Washington remarked, "it is a sturdy plant."

FINALLY, when one gets out of Athens again, the nation's troubles seem not much deeper than the Aegean Sea with its scarcity of fish, nor higher than the mountains with their paucity of woods and streams, nor more complex than the twisting stony valleys cut up into tiny farms. Greece offers a feast for the eyes and soul, with not very much left over for the belly. This was always its main "problem." But just now a new wind is rising on the borders of Greece, a wind laden with fumes, cinders and atomic particles. Technology looms, whistling, humming, promising a hurricane of progress. Greece may conceivably grow fat, it may prosper as never before, by bending to this wind and becoming an industrial nation.

Such a development would be far from easy. If it does take place, will Greece remain the Clear Land?

SHEEP graze near a winding watercourse *(left)* on the plain of Thessaly in north central Greece. Sheep and goats, the country's principal source of meat, also provide cheese, wool and hides.

WATER is siphoned into metal jugs from the town well *(opposite)* by people from a small Peloponnesian village. Many Greek towns are dependent on wells or springs for their water supplies.

Lean and Haunting Landscapes

The life of Greece is ever-changing and yet ever the same. Farming and seafaring are the principal occupations of Greeks today as they were three millennia ago. If modern Greeks have not been world leaders in art and intellectual speculation, they are still curious, quick, clever, adventurous—plainly the descendants of the men who gave western civilization its start in classical times. Amid the ancient ruins, life retains an immediacy often lost in more "advanced" countries. In few nations are the shadows of history so long, the sunlight of the present so bright.

SHINING PORT on the tiny island of Poros in the Saronic Gulf south of Athens is a summer resort for Athenians and home for hard-working fishermen *(foreground)*.

RUINED PALACE at Cnossos *(opposite)*, the center of an elegant culture which flourished on Crete about 1550 B.C., had richly painted walls and many regal corridors.

ROCK PILLARS of Meteora rise with startling abruptness above the nearby plain. Once believed to be meteors hurled by an angry god, the rocks were actually split and twisted into their fantastic shapes by the erosive power of a prehistoric sea. Offering refuge from armies contesting the fertile plain of Thessaly in the 14th Century, they became the sites of many hermitages and monasteries. One of the remaining monasteries perches atop the rock on the right.

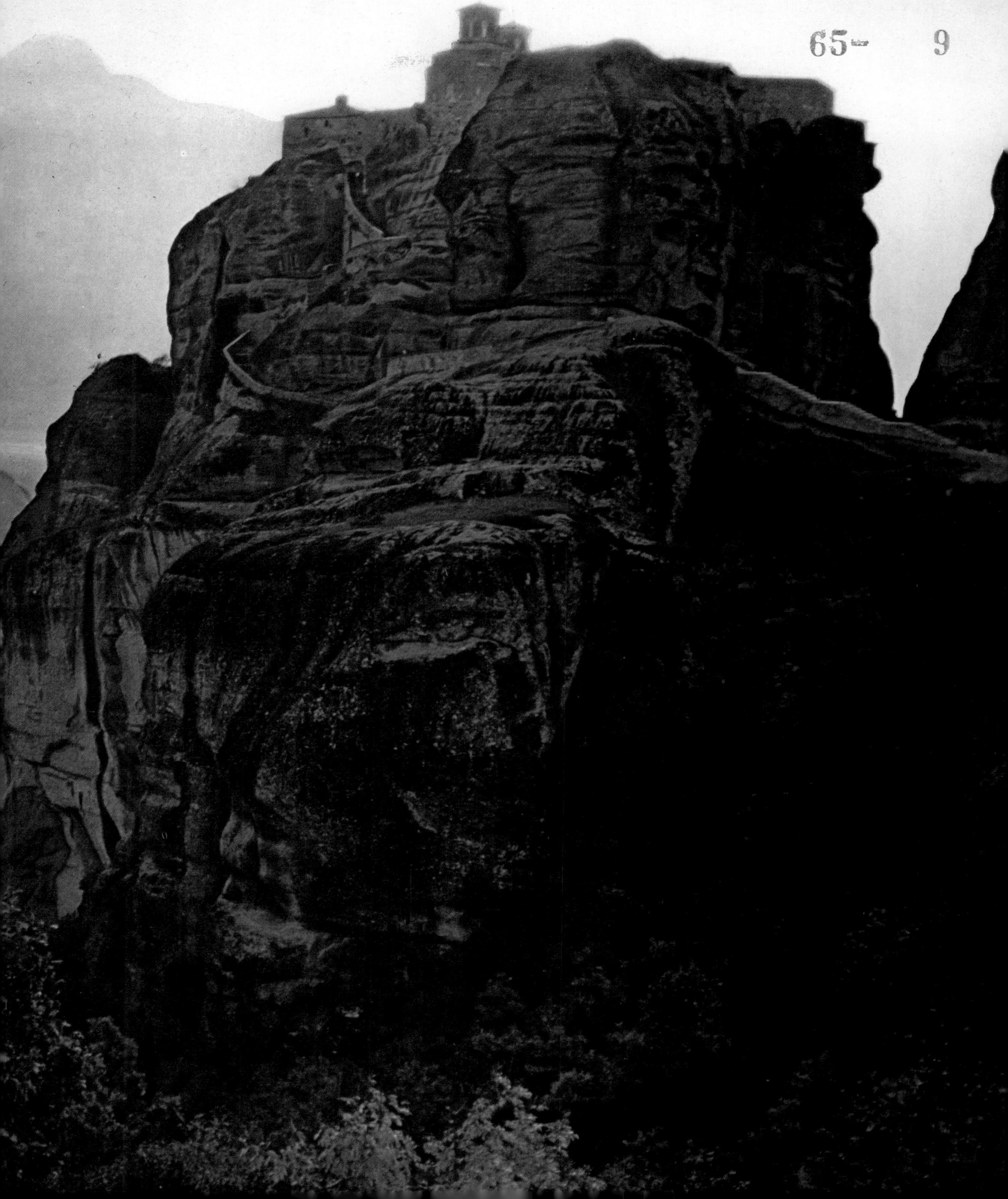

BRILLIANT ISLES in the Aegean

astound the eye with severe

landscapes and austere structures

VILLAGE CHURCH on the island of Patmos, one of the Dodecanese islands off the coast of Turkey, gleams in the strong sunlight. Once home to Saint John the Divine, it has been a place of pilgrimage for centuries.

NARROW LANE winds past the church of Saint Minas *(above)* on Thera island, one of the Cyclades chain. Island buildings are made of stone kept bright by coats of whitewash which often 'extend onto the sidewalk.

TERRACED TOWN on Siphnos *(left)* shows the typical cubistic architecture of the Cyclades islands. The hills are almost barren of trees, which were long since cut for timber and firewood, but some fruit trees remain.

SHIPWRIGHTS in a yard near Piraeus splice the bow section of an ocean-going tanker to a new middle section. Greece ranks sixth among the world's maritime nations.

DINERS eat seafood on a quay of Tourkolimano, one of the harbors of Piraeus, the port town of Athens and the busiest shipping and industrial center in the country.

FREIGHTERS load in the main harbor of Piraeus, first developed by the Athenian admiral Themistocles from 493 to 492 B.C. The Parthenon is visible in the distance.

a vigorous part of the economy, as it was in the earliest days of Athenian greatness

MASSIVE RUINS of royal tombs found at Mycenae reveal the architectural skill of the ancient Greeks, who established a powerful and artistically advanced civilization in southern Greece between about 1600 and 1200 B.C.

2

The Triumphant Beginnings

EGYPTIAN records of 4,000 years and more ago mention a mysterious "island people" as great sailors on the "green" Mediterranean. These were the people of the island of Crete. Their descendants the Minoans—King Minos' Children—frequently voyaged to Egypt. The tomb of the Pharaoh Sesostris (who died about 1880 B.C.) contained a Minoan vase. Minoan traders and ambassadors often appear in Egyptian bas-reliefs and tomb paintings. The same tall, cheery, wasp-waisted fellows were making themselves felt in all directions. Their thalassocracy, or sea empire, included settlements in Rhodes, Cyprus, Sicily and far-off Spain. But

mainland Greece also attracted their traders, who, as early as 1600 B.C., brought ornate Minoan gold work and pottery to the palace-fortresses at Thebes and Orchomenus in Boeotia, Tiryns and Mycenae in Argolis and sandy Pylos. The art and architecture, agriculture and metalwork, seamanship and enterprise of this Minoan-Greek culture constitute the first flowering of Greek civilization.

Less than a century ago virtually nothing was known of this civilization. Scholars assumed that Greek culture and history began with the Dorians, invading warrior bands from the Danube Valley who overran mainland

25

Greece, the Peloponnesus and Crete about 1100 B.C. These Dorians, it was thought, had brought with them both the Greek language and the Greek pantheon of gods. Of course there were the poems of Homer, who, writing of a time before the Dorian invasion, had pictured a graceful civilization with golden jewelry, inlaid daggers, fine manor houses, advanced cultivation and extensive trade. The scholars, however, doubted Homer's accuracy, convinced that the poet, like the early bards of other literatures, had imagined a "golden age" that never was. When Homer made his heroes speak Greek and worship Zeus and the other gods of Olympus, he seemed to be guilty of laughable anachronisms. The scholars believed that Homer was incorrectly imposing on his imaginary warriors of the 12th Century B.C. the language, religion and culture of his own post-Dorian Eighth Century.

ALL this began to change with the discovery of Troy, an ancient city in Asia Minor, almost a century ago by the German archeologist Heinrich Schliemann. Fired with the belief that Homer's story of a Greek attack on Troy was accurate, Schliemann and a crew of diggers attacked a mound of earth near the Hellespont. There they uncovered vast quantities of weapons and artifacts astonishingly like those described in the *Iliad*. The effect of their discovery was to demonstrate that Homer was very likely an accurate historian as well as a great poet.

Schliemann's subsequent excavations at Mycenae and Tiryns on the Peloponnesus, and at Orchomenus, confirmed the fact that well before the Trojan War (which took place about 1194-1184 B.C.) the people of Greece had indeed possessed a fine civilization. Further striking evidence came from Crete where an English archeologist, Sir Arthur Evans, unearthed the huge palace of King Minos at Cnossos. Many of the artifacts Evans found closely resembled those discovered at Mycenae by Schliemann. He also found tablets inscribed with two written languages. In short, here was positive proof of a high and literate civilization, both on Crete and on the Greek mainland, as early as 1600 B.C. and probably much earlier.

Still error persisted in the form of another false assumption: that the Minoans were the dominant political and cultural force and had conquered, or at least heavily colonized, the Greek mainland. Recent further excavations and scholarly reappraisal show, however, that the Minoan and mainland cultures cross-fertilized one another. If the more graceful Minoan art migrated to the mainland, mainland kings actually ruled Crete during its period of greatest brilliance.

THE capstone of this astonishing reconstruction of Greek history was provided in 1952 when a brilliant British linguist, Michael Ventris, managed to decipher for the first time the peculiar script (called "Linear B") on the tablets found by Evans at Cnossos and more recently by the American archeologist Carl Blegen at Pylos. Ventris proved, to the astonishment of the scholarly world, that this previously unreadable script was an exceedingly archaic form of Greek. Homer, it seems, was even correct about the tongue his heroes spoke.

What all this archeological and linguistic detective work adds up to is that some time after the year 2000 B.C. a Greek-speaking tribe or race, probably from the north, appeared on the Greek mainland. Eventually they had extensive dealings with the people of Crete, giving them their language, taking Cretan artistry in return. They developed a considerable maritime trade. Finally, near the end of their day of power, they fought the Trojan War that Homer describes.

Our sense of what these early Greeks were like still comes largely from Homer. He pictures a world of tiny Greek lands—Mycenae, Pylos and others—ruled by pocket kings. The nobles are not bound by man-made laws, although they recognize and respect a number of "divine" injunctions. Moreover they follow a stringent code of honor. They strive to gain what they call *aretê*—glorious excellence—by being loyal to their fellows, eloquent in counsel and, most of all, brave and victorious in battle. They kill almost at will and yet are capable of the greatest generosity, self-sacrifice and joy. Like Greeks of later times, they take delight in contest, in the use of reason and in the bloom of art.

The sons and grandsons of Homer's heroes were overwhelmed by the Dorians, and Greece's first flowering came to an end. Excavations have shown that almost all of the existing cities of the mainland except Athens were destroyed within two generations after the era of the Trojan War. These newcomers brought about a sharp decline in Greek arts and manners and a notable increase in savagery. They were puritanical and militant folk and their way of life survived here and there, notably at Sparta, well into classical times. Politically it consisted of kings and nobles, a citizen soldiery forever under arms, and miserable serfs supporting all. Instead of love and beauty, the Dorians hailed blood and booty. They brought three centuries and more of darkness to Greece. Yet the older culture survived, like a lopped stump, and eventually put out new shoots. The Argives, as Homer called them, who had fled the dull, tough Dorians settled anew on the eastern Aegean islands and along the "Ionian" coast of Asia Minor. Homer himself grew up in one such colony, perhaps on the island of Chios. The earliest known Greek scientists and philosophers were born nearby, in the city of Miletus. The cultural center of the Aegean world had first been Crete, then Mycenae and the other cities of Argolis; now it was Ionia.

THE earliest known Ionian scientist was Thales of Miletus, who offered the first natural theory of world evolution. Water, he said, is the womb of all things. Rarefied, it turns into clouds and air; condensed, it becomes ice, rock and earth. Therefore no god was needed to say "Let the dry land appear." This rational and somewhat atheistic approach to the basic problems of creation spawned a whole school of what the later Greeks called

hylozoists—those-who-think-that-matter-is-alive. Another Ionian, Anaximenes, held that air and not water is the underlying life of all.

Finally Heraclitus, also looking for a single cause of all physical phenomena, chose fire. Everything burns, he said, although often the "flames" are invisible. In other words, he believed matter was in a constant state of flux —a belief not surprising in view of modern atomic theory, although Heraclitus' poetic wording hardly fits the present fashion for abstract equations. The world, he wrote, "always was, is, and ever shall be, an ever-living fire, kindling according to fixed measure and extinguishing according to fixed measure. . . . All things are exchanged for fire, and fire for all things...."

ONE of Ionia's favorite sons was a philosopher and mathematician named Pythagoras. He seems to have been an early-day Leonardo da Vinci, a man of encyclopedic interests, but with a more mystical bent. Pythagoras set the main course of scientific speculation for all time when he made mathematics its key tool. "The nature of number," as his disciple Philolaus put it, "is to be a standard of reference, of guidance and instruction in every doubt and difficulty."

Yet the master himself was also interested in such spiritual and cloudy matters as metempsychosis, the transmigration of souls. To pursue his studies in this direction, as well as in mathematics, he followed a new Greek tide of migration westward and founded a cult at Croton, a colony on the Calabrian coast of Italy. There he taught that the soul, like the body, can be sick and that like the body it can be cured through spiritual exercises—a doctrine that looks forward both to Plato's philosophy and to Christianity.

Near Pythagoras' new home at Croton was the rival colony of Sybaris, a city whose luxury gave rise to the everlasting epithet "sybaritic." On the opposite side of the Italian peninsula lay Posidonia with its exquisite suburb Neapolis (New City), which became Naples. To

ANCIENT GREECE of around 430 B.C., with its city-states and neighboring settlements, is shown on the map above. Many boundaries were only vaguely defined. In addition to the communities shown here, the Greeks at this time also colonized parts of Spain, Italy and North Africa, and areas around the Black Sea to the east.

the south, Sicily was home to more than half a dozen Greek communities. In Italy the primitive Latins looked upon the Greek encroachment and called the intruder's domains "Magna Graecia" (after an obscure Greek tribe they called the Graeci). Thus the name "Greece" would eventually come to be.

Dorian arms, Aegean "penteconters" (50-oared galleys) and Ionian business ability now cooperated to make the Greeks invincible in the Mediterranean. Moreover, the scarcity of land at home drove whole armies of Greeks abroad. During the Sixth Century B.C., Greek holdings along the coasts of the known world were more extensive than during the Minoan heyday of 1,000 years before. In the far west, the Greeks first colonized what would one day become the French Riviera and the Spanish Costa Brava. At the eastern limits of the known

world they established equally prosperous and pretty Black Sea outposts: Trebizond, and Colchis, where the hero Jason sought the Golden Fleece, and the Crimean city of Heraclea.

During the Sixth Century B.C. a new force swept Asia and began pressing upon Europe. Under mighty Cyrus and his descendants, the Persian empire swelled beyond any earthly kingdom that the world had known. The state concept which these proud Aryans forced upon their new subjects was simple indeed and not altogether evil. It called for king worship, stiff taxes and internal peace, and for gathering a diversity of cultures into political unity. Hellenic ideals were just the opposite. The Greeks worshiped no mere man, loathed paying tribute and relished small wars. Both at home and abroad they banded together in autonomous city-states where "everyone knew everyone else." This seemed essential to their strongly individualistic way of life. The city-states tried all sorts of government. Most of them knew internal turmoil and an unending clamor for special privileges and individual rights, but they were independent. In addition the Greeks had, as the Persian subjects did not, a common language and a single unforced religion. In other words, they proudly practiced political diversity within a cultural unity.

IONIA fell to the Persians. So did Thrace. Thebes and other Boeotian cities leaned their way. It seemed only a matter of time before all Greece, divided as it was, would go under. But Athens stood firm. The city was to prove both a stumbling block to the invading East and a seedbed of our own civilization.

Athens was a city-state of a rather peculiar kind. By conquest it had incorporated close to a dozen surrounding villages with all their lands. But some sage Athenian leader (Theseus, tradition held) had made the conquered villagers full Athenian citizens instead of slaves. These citizens had rejected royal fuss and flummery as early as 1088 B.C. The monarchy was succeeded by the rule of an aristocracy headed by an archon, or regent. This arrangement gave way in turn to the rule of an oligarchy—government by all the more wealthy and powerful citizens. The authorities consisted of all those whose estates produced more than 500 measures of grain, wine or olive oil in a year. Then came the knights, men rich enough to go mounted and fully armed into battle. Last in privilege were the farmers and craftsmen. Below their level, legal rights dwindled away to nothing. The poor could even be sold into slavery by creditors for nonpayment of debts.

Under this system the rich naturally got richer, greedier and more scared, while the poor got poorer, meaner and more furious. Something similar was happening in other city-states, which generally suffered revolutions alternating with the rule of "tyrants," or popular demagogues. Athens was spared that for the moment. About the year 594 B.C. rich and poor alike called on a wise merchant named Solon to arbitrate between them. Solon instantly freed all those who had been enslaved for nonpayment of debts, made such enslavement illegal in the future, and canceled all debts outstanding. Moreover he broke up the great estates. Then he wrote a constitution designed to stand for "a hundred years."

In order to prevent backsliding, Solon ruled that during civic disputes anyone who so much as remained neutral on a constitutional question must forfeit citizenship. Solon's constitution gave political status for the first time to a fourth class composed of sailors and free workmen. Most important: it called for judicial assemblies, on important occasions, open to *all* the citizens. Women were barred, still, from citizenship. Slaves and foreign residents had practically no rights. Nobody would call Solon's creation a utopia. Yet with Solon democracy was born.

AFTER Solon, Athens passed through a benevolent tyranny (imposed by Pisistratus) which kept at least the forms of constitutional government. Later it liberalized Solon's constitution under the leadership of Cleisthenes. The city had become an international trader in painted pottery, wine, olive oil and arms. Athens' adventurous merchants roamed everywhere in the Mediterranean. Moreover Athens' armor manufacturers gave military dominance to the hoplite, or heavily armed foot soldier. The mounted knights had long since faded as protectors of the realm. Athens now depended for defense upon every able-bodied citizen between the ages of 18 and 60. And they *were* able-bodied, astonishingly so, since most male Athenians spent a part of every day at open-air "gymnasiums," boxing, wrestling and running.

In the decade after 500 B.C. these vigorous and adventurous Athenians, along with the people of the Euboean island city of Eretria, actively aided a revolt of the Ionians against their Persian rulers and laid waste the city of Sardes. Tiring of these depredations, the Persians sent an attack force across the Aegean and slaughtered or enslaved the people of Eretria. Next the Persians beached their boats at Marathon, a calm, smiling bay in Athenian territory. About 10,000 Athenians drew up to oppose them, together with 1,000 allies from the town of Plataea. The Persian invaders outnumbered them at least two to one.

The Spartans refused to send reinforcements even though a young man named Pheidippides ran the whole 140 miles from Athens to Sparta —thus our word "marathon" for a long foot race—to deliver a plea for help. Without Spartan aid resistance appeared hopeless. But to judge by the fate of Eretria, the enemy was implacable, merciless. Should the Greeks do battle, or retreat? Disaster threatened either way. The Greek commanders voted—six to five in favor of attack.

Their thin line lowered lances and charged a full mile, on the run, down into the Persian horde. The Greeks possessed no archers and no cavalry, but their spears crashed through the wicker shields of the invaders. Slowly the Persians were driven back upon their ships. The invaders drew off badly mauled, leaving almost a third of their soldiers dead on the field.

BUT did the slight repulse for Persia really matter so much? Old-school histories tend to overemphasize the work of war, because battles seem so reassuringly definite. Yet as a rule the political and economic aspects of history have more lasting effects than the military. All the same, the importance attending the Battle of Marathon can hardly be exaggerated. It was not a major engagement; however, two continents and totally opposed sets of ideals clashed at Marathon. Athens' seemingly miraculous defense signaled the start of a long, slow decline for Asia and the beginning of European leadership upon the world stage. More important, it showed that free citizens can face down a far superior force of kings' men. The echoes of Marathon have yet to die away.

The supreme test came 10 years after Marathon, when the new Persian emperor, Xerxes, mounted a full-scale land and sea invasion which hurled the combined might of Asia against tiny Greece. At Thermopylae, Leonidas and his brave 300 Spartans performed a heroic holding action. But the Persian host came on over their dead bodies. Athens was put to the torch. The Greek navy, chiefly Athenian, was bottled up in the Straits of Salamis. Xerxes ordered his bronze-beaked armada to attack and sink the Greek power for all time. Enthroned upon a cliff, he prepared to gloat over the slaughter. As Byron was to write:

> *A king sate on the rocky brow*
> *Which looks o'er sea-born Salamis;*
> *And ships, by thousands, lay below,*
> *And men in nations;—all were his!*
> *He counted them at break of day—*
> *And when the sun set where were they?*

They were mostly at the bottom, put there by Greek heroism and superior seamanship. Xerxes beat a hasty retreat out of Europe. And like flowers springing up after a storm, a new glory grew in Greece.

Throughout the mid-Fifth Century B.C., every aspect of Greek endeavor shone. Athens, laid in hopeless ruins by the Persians, rebuilt itself and led the way. The city was wealthy now, controlling most of the Aegean islands and constantly increasing its overseas trade. But instead of burdening itself with excessive material luxury, the city splurged on things of the spirit. Back of this choice stood Pericles, the personal friend of almost every great Greek in his time. As Athens' ruler-by-persuasion, Pericles is the great figure of this golden moment, this climax of the classical age.

By his day the Assembly of Athens had grown to about 43,000 adult male citizens. This, astonishingly enough, was Athens' legislative body. Judges and bureaucrats were chosen each year by lot. The city's highest authority was an executive body of 10 generals elected for one year only. Here was democracy with a vengeance. Naturally political cliques and clubs abounded. Problems of special privilege loomed large in the assembly and were constantly being tested in the courts. But Pericles believed in this democracy with all his heart. He did nothing to change the rules in his own favor.

Meanwhile he was re-elected almost continuously for 31 years (461-430 B.C.) to the executive body of generals. He made this foothold a personal throne, for he ruled as firmly as any monarch—by pure persuasion. There was danger in the paradox. With Pericles for a pilot, Athens' democratic ship of state sailed smoothly. Without him it afterward sailed into tumultuous, capricious and cruel adventures.

Pericles' government was long on positive projects and gratifyingly short on restrictions. Import and export duties were a hospitable 1 per cent. Athenian sons were required to support their aged parents—if those same parents had taught them a trade. In a city addicted to litigation, he arranged that jury duty be well paid. Food prices he controlled, on the ground that nobody should be permitted to profit unreasonably from another's hunger.

His most imaginative stroke was to call a Panhellenic conference in 448 B.C. aimed at creating a peaceful and permanent federation of the Greek city-states. This could have been done, conceivably, as it was done so much later in America. However, Sparta's boycott spoiled the plan. Athens remained the proud but lonely and uneasy queen of an Aegean island empire, held together by its naval power alone.

RIVAL forces on the mainland and the Peloponnesus—Thebes, Corinth and mighty Sparta—first envied, then feared and finally hated Athens. Pericles had raised the city up too high and made it too proud. In the year 431 B.C. the Peloponnesian League, led by Sparta, marched against it. The Peloponnesian War was on its way to ruining all Greece.

Thucydides, the immortal historian of that war, makes plain his belief that Pericles could have won it. But the great plague which decimated Athens shortly after the war had begun carried off the city's leader. The memory of him soon was blurred with present horror. Demagogues took charge. The first blossomings of western culture withered and went to seed. Yet just as Pericles had stood for an actual culture triumphant, so Plato in the next generation would stand for an ideal of philosophic culture.

To both Pericles and Plato, wisdom seemed the height of value. But wisdom as understood by them was oceans removed from the quiz-kid mentality. In classical times it never meant a large, laboriously acquired body of knowledge but rather an intelligent way of life. The Greeks believed that the true poles of wisdom were given at Delphi, in the inscriptions *Know Thyself* and *Nothing in Excess*. These seemed enough, and surely they are tough enough.

IN every discipline and every art, Pericles had fostered keen public rivalry. He lavishly sponsored sports events and festivals of music, dance and poetry, setting aside for them no less than 60 official holidays. Presiding over the greatest theater that the world has known, he offered to pay the public the equivalent of jury-duty fees to attend it. Thus he made sure that rich and poor alike witnessed the performances.

In fact the chief business of the Athenian state at its best was to help create a wiser, more virtuous and happy citizen. The ideal is known to us, of course, but how few nations have ever really taken steps to promote cultural and spiritual excellence in their people! As for happiness, it would seem within most people's reach, given the right circumstances, and yet how few people admit to being happy! Sometimes it seems that happiness is just a wish. The Greeks had a better idea.

They thought of happiness as a living, natural thing—a birthright, providing you strove to be worthy of it. The playwright Sophocles even went so far as to state (in his *Antigone*) that one who has lost the sense of joy is already as good as dead. The Greeks saw happiness as something quite apart from leisure, love or money; something which could never be earned, nor bought, nor even given away. Happiness meant one thing only. It meant doing one's best under highly encouraging circumstances.

By this definition, the citizens of Periclean Athens may have been the happiest yet.

SEEDY SLUMS surround an Athenian mother as she feeds her children *(left)* outside their shack. Athens has begun an ambitious slum clearance program, but shanty villages still house the least fortunate of the urban poor.

GLORIOUS TEMPLE, the floodlit Parthenon *(opposite)* gleams atop the Acropolis, towering over the buildings and the bright lights of modern, mundane Athens. Downtown Athens is a potpourri of architectural styles.

Athens, a City Unawed by Its History

The presence of its exciting past adds a lyric dimension to the prose of modern Athens. A modern capital city with traffic jams and office buildings, and with its share of advertising posters and slums, Athens also includes remnants of the great epoch when it was the first center of western culture. The busy, practical modern city is not, however, overawed by its history; rather it is determined to make itself once again into an important center of culture and trade.

THE MODERN CITY *combines the virtues and vices of today with the leisurely,*

informal ways of an earlier time

SUNNY ESPLANADE in the center of Athens is a maze of tables and chairs belonging to the many cafés and food shops which surround Syntagma (Constitution) Square.

SLEEK APARTMENTS line a sunny hillside street in Athens *(left)* with a good view of Mount Lykabettos, named for the wolves that lived on its slopes in ancient times.

BRIGHT KIOSK houses a telephone as well as a bewildering variety of goods, from cigarettes and newspapers to drugs, fountain pens and flashlight batteries.

Bettors put their money down at the small Phaleron Race Course near Athens, where girls do the work of pari-mutuel machines.

OPEN-AIR MARKET selling fruits and flowers *(opposite)* flourishes even in the fashionable Kolonaki section of Athens. Greek fruits are famous for their excellence.

PACKED FIELD of horses *(below)* thunders by the judges' stand at the Phaleron race track. The horse players get a fine view of both the Parthenon and Mount Lykabettos.

STONE MAIDENS still stand supporting a porch roof of the Erechtheum, a
complex temple opposite the Parthenon on Athens' Acropolis. Completed
around 405 B.C., it was damaged
in 1827 but has since been restored.

3

A Golden
Moment

SALMON swim instinctively home from the
sea and climb ancestral rivers threading
back to the streams that gave them birth. A
trip to Athens can be like that. It means going
home to the spawning grounds of western
culture—a 25-century return. Many classicists
have dreaded the trip, and not a few have managed to avoid making it. They feared that
modern Athens would destroy their imaginative vision of the ancient one. It is true that
Athens shares the faults of all great cities today. Even its celebrated sunlight, so caressing
and so crystalline, is somewhat bleared with
smoke and gasoline fumes now. Not even the
most devoted children of Athens will deny that
in some ways the city resembles a writhing asphalt octopus. Yet in the modern city's midst,
the Acropolis with its Parthenon still stands as a
shining citadel of an ideal.

Intellectual and spiritual freedom are the
roots of this ideal—freedom of inquiry and
freedom of human sympathy. Its blossom is
political and cultural—the power to cooperate
within the bounds of reason and thereby build
a glorious society.

The citadel of the ideal has been invaded of
late by unfeeling restorers. In bright sunshine
the Acropolis ruins now appear face-lifted,

39

stiff. By night in summer they become a tourist show. Canned music, canned sentiments and colored searchlights combine to swathe the nighttime marble in vulgarity. But on full moon nights the Acropolis still is left alone. Those are the magic times to take it in.

Ascending the templed hill by moonlight one seems to be entering a new and better-ordered plane of existence. At right the tiny Ionic temple of the so-called Wingless Victory (Nike) perches, exquisite, overlooking a precipice. A marble goddess who once resided in the temple's balustrade was bending down to untie her sandal before approaching her mistress, Athena. She can still be seen, unutterably graceful despite her occupation, in the Acropolis Museum.

The massive gateway of the Acropolis is itself a triumph of mind over matter. Or, in more prosaic terms, of engineering skill over gravity. The level courses of this entrance seem to contradict the steep rocky slope on which they stand. Through the 24 columns that make up the gates one first glimpses the Parthenon suspended ahead like a grove of moonlight. Down to the left hovers the third of the Acropolis' four remaining major structures, the Erechtheum, an irregular Ionic temple with its southern porch upheld by six columns shaped in the likeness of lovely women. Yet the abstract splendor of the Parthenon draws one irresistibly uphill.

The columns, which seemed so like stone tree trunks in the distance, now are more like waterfalls or fountains of light. The broad flutings scooped from their sides heighten this

HUGE STATUE of Athena, sculpted by Phidias, stood 38 feet high and dominated the Parthenon's hall. Made of ivory and gold over a wooden core, it is thought to have been destroyed some time in the Fifth Century A.D.

effect. In Egypt the flutings of columns are convex, to imitate bundled papyrus. Here they are concave, as if to suggest the flow of air or water over living stone. Stars shine where the roof once was. Glimmering far off in the distance is huge, patient Mount Pentelikon, where the marble for these buildings was quarried.

The Parthenon was sacred to Athena, the city's virgin goddess of wisdom. The temple stands empty and more than half destroyed, yet still has power to change the heart. Men breathe deeper here. No one has ever discovered the system of measurements that will exactly fit the Parthenon. This "geometry in marble" was not shaped to measure, but to measured thought. All its long straight lines were bent a bit, to bring them into harmony with the round eye of man. Hundreds of citizens anciently labored here to the chinking of chisels in a swirl of marble dust. Since scores of separate small contractors were at work, sometimes one to a column, the temple shows hundreds of tiny variations. That is one reason why it defies exact proportional analysis and why its beauty resembles nature's own. For here, just as in a forest glade, one finds numerous small diversities within unity.

The Parthenon belonged to every Athenian, and rightly so. Neither nature nor wealth nor brilliant leaders nor even great artists alone can make a Parthenon, although all four are necessary. Such achievements require many men working together—"wondrous men," in Sophocles' phrase, "masters of speech and windswift thought and the ordering of cities." Such were the citizens of Athens in the time of Pericles. The city was no bigger than Omaha, Nebraska, yet within a few generations Athens developed thinkers and writers and artists who changed the whole world forever. Dozens of them are still remembered and revered, each man for some previously unheard-of epochal accomplishment.

Classical Athens achieved a golden moment in the journey of mankind. Like one's own happiest days, it merits fond remembrance now and then. Imagine, for example, the scene that may have occurred on a summer morning in the year 438 B.C., when the Parthenon was dedicated.

. . . The high Acropolis gleams under a brilliant blue sky. A procession is winding slowly up from the city below. The crowd already on the hilltop is casually festive and alight with honored guests, waiting for the ceremonies to start. No one knows precisely who was there, but the list of people must include most, if not all, of the great Athenians of the day.

Burly, aging Phidias stands mopping his bald head while chatting nervously with Ictinus and Callicrates, the Parthenon's architects. Phidias has charge of all public works in Athens. He designed the Parthenon's sculptures and created the 38-foot statue of Athena inside the temple. Athena's hair, helmet, tunic and shield are all of fine gold; her flesh is ivory. When the great eastern doors swing open, the morning sun will pour in upon her so that she shines like fire and snow. Phidias is the first to have attempted such lapidary work on so heroic a scale. He has put the statue together so cunningly that the joints cannot be seen. The gold alone weighs more than a ton. In case of emergency it can and will be removed, for the goddess is also the state gold reserve.

Will the citizens condemn or admire his work? Phidias' fears on that score are understandably slight. But he has another cause for concern: rumor whispers that he has short-changed the goddess by keeping a fraction of her golden raiment for his own use. Because of this irresponsible charge, Phidias will eventually face a sentence of banishment.

Sophocles sits off to one side, in the dappled shade of an olive tree, gravely disputing a point of mythology with his intense, tangle-bearded colleague Euripides. Their passion is the drama. Through their tragedies they are adding a human dimension to the might of Greek myths and the beauty of Greek music and dance. Sophocles alone will have written and staged more than 120 tragedies before he dies. Yet like most of the great Greeks he practices many professions. Only 16 when Athens defeated Persia at Salamis, Sophocles led the youths' chorus in the victory dance. At about the age of 20 he went on the stage, playing the part of a girl, Nausicaa, in one of his own productions. In his forties he undertook various temple duties as a priest. In his fifties he was an admiral at the Battle of Samos. And now he has just completed an honorable tour of duty as Athens' secretary of the treasury.

Euripides, Sophocles' companion and chief rival, is a very different sort. A recluse by Athenian standards, he often absents himself

---

THOUGHTS ON MAN AND NATURE

What the Greeks thought of themselves and their world is indicated by the quotations given below. It is quite possible that all of these quotations would have been familiar to the men who are described in the accompanying chapter.

Single is the race, single / Of men and gods; / From a single mother we both draw breath.   -Pindar

To think is the greatest virtue and wisdom consists of speaking what is true and acting in obedience to nature.   -Heraclitus

For a man health is the first and best possession, / Second best to be born with shapely beauty, / And the third is wealth honestly won, / Fourth are the days of youth spent in delight with friends.   -Attic drinking song

To describe the Athenians' character in a word, one might truly say that they were born into the world to take no rest themselves and to give none to others.   -Thucydides

for weeks at a time to work in a book-lined sea cave on the wild island of Salamis. Euripides is profoundly religious in feeling, profoundly skeptical in mind. There can be no more explosive combination, in a genius, than this one. It makes his plays enigmatic, shocking, sometimes even scandalous to Athens. Yet the citizens attend his offerings year after year. Just now, Euripides is working on a play with a particularly startling invocation: *Oh, Zeus, if there be a Zeus, for I know of him only by report. . . .*

QUITE possibly Herodotus has arranged to be in Athens on this historic day. His *Persian Wars* is the first general history ever written, yet future ages will agree in calling it the best as well. Almost 2,000 years hence it will begin to find publishers. Schoolboys will be forced to memorize bits of it. And finally the *Persian Wars* will even metamorphose into paperback editions, alighting in drugstores and air terminals around the world. At present, however, the history exists only in Herodotus' own manuscript, which he uses as notes for his profession: travel-lecturing. This work well suits the spry Ionian and adopted son of Athens. It enables him to satisfy his warm, insatiable curiosity about the whole known world. In his lectures, Herodotus keeps jogging fellow Greeks out of provincial ruts, preaching tolerance and telling them with half a wink that everything they know really comes from Egypt. He also serves Athens on occasion as a foreign-policy expert, and for this the Athenians have awarded him a small fortune.

Certainly Thucydides must be present this morning. One can picture the future general and historian standing by Herodotus' bench. He may have been allowed to read a little of the old spellbinder's long manuscript. In any case he will grow up to rival it and add a frontier of his own to the writing of history. Thucydides' *Peloponnesian War* will be the first full-scale attempt at objective moral, military and political accounting. Moreover, it too will live as long as western literature survives.

Those grizzled beards and wrinkled brows in the visitors' stand belong to the Sophists, or "teachers of wisdom." Athens welcomes these wandering professors and makes them feel at home. Chief among them is Protagoras, propounder of the disturbing new doctrine that "man is the measure of all things." This radical humanism has earned him praise and blame in about equal portions, as it always will.

With Protagoras sit two other Sophists, Prodicus and Hippias, and the astronomer Meton, all men who are devoted to objective measurement. Meton is bent on reforming the Athenian lunar calendar to bring it into line with the solar year. He will do it, and set part of the framework for modern conceptions of space and time. As for Prodicus, he is assisting Protagoras to construct the first systematic grammar of the Greek language as spoken in Attica. As a result of Athens' political supremacy, its dialect has become the most important one in Greece. In a generation, the Attic dialect will serve as the basis for a common tongue, or *koinê dialektos,* which absorbs all the older, local variants. So the work Prodicus is now doing will help to establish the thoroughly articulated language which will prove powerful enough to bear the thoughts of Plato and Aristotle and the mysteries of the New Testament and, incidentally, will survive up to the present day. So Prodicus labors for the not yet born.

HIPPIAS is the first recorded prophet of a back-to-nature movement. He preaches self-sufficiency, makes his own clothes, grows his own food and inveighs against Athenian city slickers. He is learned but arrogant and frivolous, and he will help give the Sophists a bad name, which will be preserved in the derogatory word "sophistry." Meanwhile, he looks backward. Having obtained from the priests at Olympia a list of the victors in past Olympic Games, he is using it to order Greek chronology. Fortunately the list of past victors dates all the way back to what will one day be called 776 B.C., giving Hippias a convenient structure for a considerable chunk of history.

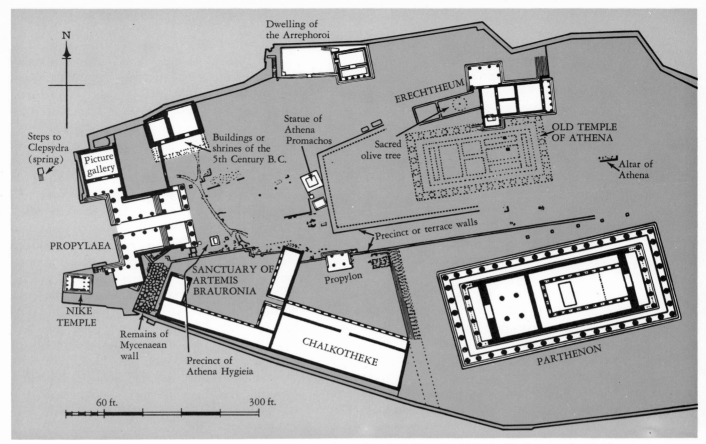

PLAN OF THE ACROPOLIS shows the buildings and principal exterior statuary which adorned the main section of the plateau in the Fifth Century B.C. Today only four of the buildings remain: the Parthenon, the Erechtheum, the Propylaea, or entrance gates *(left)*, and, near the Propylaea, the tiny temple of Athena Nike.

His work will be carried on by Timaeus, who will date things according to "Olympiads."

The artists who have come today have chosen a natural outcropping of rock from which to view the coming dedication. Among them is Agatharcus, set designer for the Athenian Theater, who talks eagerly as he draws straight lines along the air with his thumb. In the course of his struggles to create an illusion of distance upon the stage, Agatharcus has hit on the laws of perspective. As he explains the mathematics involved, his friends nod politely, stifling their yawns. Agatharcus' discovery will be forgotten and 2,000 years will pass before its rediscovery by Italian artists during the early Renaissance.

Polygnotus the urn painter, one of two famous Athenian artists of that name, is eying the girls as usual. At work he will re-create them,

drawing directly on his vases with a paint-filled goose quill or fine brush. Polygnotus can draw a dance or a battle or a feast just as simply as singing. His lighthearted and low-cost manufactures are the joy of housewives all the way from Babylon to Barcelona. They soon break, yet fragments of them are to survive the ages underground. Dug up and pieced together once again, they will become the prize possessions of museums and millionaires. Minor creations such as these outshine the "masterpieces" made in more tired times. Meanwhile the light in Polygnotus' eye conveys a message very like the one in Keats's "Ode on a Grecian Urn"—*"Beauty is truth, truth beauty,"—that is all / Ye know on earth, and all ye need to know.*

Doctor Hippocrates stands conversing with a barefoot friend. For years medicine in Greece has been reserved for initiates in the cult of

A Golden Moment

Asclepius. Traditionally passed on from priest to neophyte—often from father to son—it stems from old Egyptian sources. But Hippocrates is changing all that; he means to bring medicine out into the open and give it a more rational and empirical basis. To this end he makes objectively descriptive notes on interesting cases— successful or not—and circulates them among his colleagues. Also he is writing treatises on various climates and diets in relation to health. He takes in students from all over Greece, only requiring that they swear to maintain a certain ethical code: the Hippocratic Oath.

JUST now the good doctor smooths back his hair and fumbles for words while his barefoot, philosophic friend smiles encouragement. Although only 31 years old, Socrates is already much loved and much feared. He keeps pushing questions at people, hard questions and seemingly useless ones. Socrates' passion is the care and training of the human soul. The men that he is destined to affect most deeply— Plato and Xenophon among them—have not yet come into the world, but when they do he will be prepared. This morning Socrates wants to know whether or not any of Hippocrates' prescriptions for the body apply to the soul as well. His back turned squarely on the gleaming new Parthenon, his eyes shining deep in his homely round head, Socrates presses for a solid answer and will not be satisfied.

The scientific fraternity stands a little apart from the crowd, pretending not to notice either the suspicious glances of old people or the frankly staring children. Anaxagoras, the city's leading scientific intellect, has shocked patriotic Athens by proclaiming that the one place where he feels at home is not in their beloved city but in the night sky. On top of that unwelcome riddle he piles others, yet more fantastic. The sun, says Anaxagoras, is not a god but a molten rock many times larger than the Peloponnesus. Shooting stars are also rocks, torn from other planets and afire with the speed of their fall.

For expressing such ideas as these, Anaxagoras is often accused of "impiety." Yet he goes further still. All things, he maintains, are really composed of seeds: invisible corpuscles which swarmed chaotically until the *nous*, or ordering principle of the universe, gave them direction, thus forming earth and air, plants and men. Some of his colleagues disagree. They speak of "primal elements" having the place of seeds. A certain Democritus of Abdera, they report, has reduced the world to atoms (*atoma* in Greek, meaning literally "uncuttables") and the void.

But this is no moment for abstract speculation. The procession has reached the hilltop. Here come the young men, sun-tanned, practically nude, astride high-prancing horses tightly reined. Here come the maidens of the city, with the breezes curling their tunics and lifting their hair. They carry wine, olive branches, honey cakes and a new embroidered robe for Athena, the maiden goddess. Here come the city fathers, motionless, in chariots—looming, lowering, full-bearded men. And here at last comes Pericles, Athens' uncrowned king. He is lithe, broad-shouldered, medium tall. His face is handsome, impassive and yet suggestive of strong emotion held in check. He briskly mounts the steps of the Parthenon and turns to face the crowd.

Nobody knows what Pericles actually said on this occasion. Several of his speeches have come down to us, however, recorded by Thucydides. And a part of one of them would have perfectly suited the dedication of the Parthenon. In it Pericles gives the human foundations of Athens' greatness:

> *For we are lovers of the beautiful, yet simple in our tastes, and we cultivate the mind without loss of manliness. . . . For we have a peculiar power of thinking before we act and then acting too, whereas other men are courageous from ignorance but hesitant upon reflection. . . . I say that Athens is the school of Hellas. . . . And we shall assuredly not be without witnesses; there are mighty monuments to our power which will make us the wonder of this and succeeding ages. . . . For the whole earth is the sepulcher of famous men.*

Shining softly in the calm moonlight, the weathered columns of the Parthenon frame the gaudy lights of modern nighttime Athens.

Noble Evocations of a Magnificent Era

The temples of Greece bring vividly alive the contradictions of the great age which gave them birth. In the stately march of their simple columns the visitor can sense the ancient Greek passion for rational order. And in the groves and on the rocky eminences where the temples stand can also be sensed the other, less orderly part of the Greek temper, the part that listened to the shrieks of oracles and, through war, tore its own magnificent civilization to pieces.

ISOLATED TEMPLE at Bassae, high in the mountains of Arcadia, is one of the best preserved of all Greek shrines. Its fine frieze, however, was acquired during the 19th Century by the British Museum in London. The temple was built of gray limestone between about 450 and 425 B.C. by Ictinus, one of the designers of the Parthenon.

STARK REMAINS of the Temple of Apollo at Corinth crown a hill near the narrow isthmus which connects central Greece and the Peloponnesus. Of simple design, the temple was built a century before the Parthenon.

LONELY COLUMNS stand on the high promontory of Cape Sounion on the southernmost tip of Attica, south of Athens. Dedicated to Poseidon, the god of the sea, the temple was the last thing seen by outbound sailors.

SACRED GROVE shelters the ruins (*opposite*) of the building at Olympia, where feasts were held during the original Olympic Games and where an altar held an eternal flame.

REMOTE SANCTUARY lies near the road leading to the Temple of Apollo at Delphi, to which people from all over Greece came to ask questions of the Delphic Oracle.

49

An old print shows the Parthenon during the days of Turkish rule, when a mosque stood amid the temple's ruins. After Greece became

independent, the mosque and the nearby buildings were torn down.

4

The
Sleep
of Centuries

THE disaster which overtook Xerxes' Persian expedition against Greece in 480 B.C. had pointed a clear enough moral. As the playwright Aeschylus put it: "Sow arrogance, and reap a tasseled field of doom!" Thucydides, three generations later, drew the same moral from the Peloponnesian War. But this time it was Greek arrogance that brought doom to Greece. Athens and Sparta were perhaps equally to blame for this terrible conflict which brought the golden moment to an end. Each hated and feared the other. Each insisted that its own form of government and its own leadership must prevail. As a result, Thucydides recorded, "practically the whole Hellenic world was convulsed."

Athens with its island empire became locked in combat with the Spartan alliance. In the crisis of war, all reason and moderation fled; Athenian greatness died long before the war itself was over. All this Thucydides made brutally clear, both for his own time and as a lesson to future generations. In Rex Warner's lucid English translation:

"To fit in with the change of events, words, too, had to change their usual meanings. What used to be described as a thoughtless act of aggression was now regarded as the courage one would expect to find in a party member; to think of the future and wait was merely another way of saying one was a coward; any idea of moderation was just an attempt to disguise one's unmanly character; ability to understand a question from all sides meant that one was totally unfitted for action. Fanatical enthusiasm was the mark of a real man, and to plot against an enemy behind his back was perfectly legitimate self-defense. Anyone who held violent opinions could always be trusted, and anyone who objected to them became a suspect. . . . As a result of these revolutions, there was a general deterioration of character throughout the Greek world. The simple way of looking at things, which is so much the mark of a noble nature, was regarded as a ridiculous quality and soon ceased to exist. Society had become divided into two ideologically hostile camps, and each side viewed the other with suspicion. As for ending this state of affairs, no guarantee could be given that would be trusted, no oath sworn that people would fear to break; everyone had come to the conclusion that it was hopeless to expect a permanent settlement and so, instead of being able to feel confident in others, they devoted their energies to providing against being injured themselves."

Classical Greece might have given even more to mankind by its violent death than in its life —if only this terrible object lesson had been taken to heart. But it never has been. Technically Sparta at last won the Peloponnesian War since Athens capitulated in 404 B.C. Everyone

PORTRAIT OF ALEXANDER was used on coins issued by one of his successors, as shown in this woodcut by a 17th Century Italian artist. The ram's horn over the ear signifies the conqueror's self-assumed divine status.

lost, however. And Athens, a democracy with everything to lose, lost everything.

In the year 399 B.C. Athens declared its own spiritual bankruptcy by "executing" Socrates. His crime was that he was a thinking patriot. Socrates' profound devotion to Athens had made him an especially brave and honored soldier. It also caused him to speak out frankly when the city lost its way, urging virtue even upon villains. So they voted death to him. He could have escaped the sentence by "recanting" or self-exile. Instead he stayed as firm in court as he had in battle, for the city's sake.

Socrates' response to his own condemnation was good humored but straight to the mark. "If you expect to stop denunciation of your wrong way of life by putting people to death," he said, "there is something amiss with your reasoning. This way of escape is neither possible nor creditable. The best and easiest way is not to stop the mouths of others, but to make yourselves as good men as you can. . . ."

Classical Greek life—particularly in Athens—had been a kind of tripod structure made up of politics, thought and art. But with the war and the judicial murder of Socrates, this tripod fell apart. Thought and art of course survived the breakup. They still flourished astonishingly. Politics, however, declined to the level of provincial squabbling and jobbery. Into the vacuum thus created, alien powers rode. Politically, Greece subsided to the fretful slumber of a state enslaved. This slumber was to last for centuries, while Macedonian, Roman, Byzantine, Frank and Turk marched and wheeled across the counterpane.

The Macedonians, warlike brothers of the Greeks from the north, came first, in the mid-Fourth Century B.C. Their king was shrewd, drunken Philip. He subverted the city-states of the south mainly by threats and bribes. The orator Demosthenes saw what was happening and warned Athens in his brilliant but apparently unpersuasive *Philippics*. (They became required reading for schoolboys from Marcus Aurelius to Winston Churchill.) Rhetorical questions were Demosthenes' favorite artillery: "Is Philip dead? Nay but he is ill. And what is that to you? For if this king die you soon will raise up a second Philip by your apathy!"

WHEN Philip was assassinated, Greece awakened for just a moment to its old freedoms and tried to reassert them. But then Philip's son, Alexander of Macedon, 20 and terrible, came down with his avalanche of spears. Thebes was utterly destroyed—except for one dwelling, the supposed birthplace of the poet Pindar. Alexander liked poetry. The boy let Athens stand as well, perhaps out of respect for his old tutor, Aristotle, who had settled there. Having made Greek subjection sure, he turned east against the last of the Persian kings, conquering all the way to India. Alexander founded some 20 cities bearing his name. One especially, on the Nile Delta, still lives. Far and wide he established cultural (but not political) replicas of the Greek city-state.

Alexander's assumption of "divine right," however, was Persian or Egyptian and the opposite of Greek. At the Olympic Games of 324 B.C., as Diodorus Siculus records, heralds proclaimed the conqueror's polite "request" for deification. To which the Spartan delegation laconically replied: "We agree that Alexander should call himself a god if he wishes."

Alexander's goal had been to bring East and West into harmony. For a few years he seemed likely to succeed. But after his early death the empire fell apart, dividing roughly along continental lines. The province of Egypt fell to General Ptolemy, the Near East to the Seleucid dynasts and Greece to a succession of native warlords. The most ambitious of these last was Pyrrhus, the king of Epirus, who undertook to contest Europe's future with Rome. In 279 B.C. Pyrrhus won a bloody and negatively

famous battle on Italian soil. Viewing the carnage, he remarked to his officers: "Another victory like this and I am lost!" Not long afterward, Rome annexed Macedonia, making it a province of the Roman Empire. It took over the rest of Greece in 146 B.C.

Corinth attempted revolt and was systematically leveled with the ground. Culturally, Greece was still a great power, but it had been reduced to impotence in politics and war alike. Now it served as a convenient battleground for others. The Roman rivals Pompey and Caesar fought each other on the Thessalian plain. Off the west coast near Actium, Caesar Augustus' fleet put the great but passionate Marc Antony and his Egyptian queen, Cleopatra, to flight. In the time of Tiberius, as the Roman historian Tacitus relates, a Roman governor named Piso stood up at Athens and contemptuously reviled the entire citizenry. He blamed his predecessor for "having treated with excessive courtesy not the people of Athens, who indeed had been exterminated by repeated disasters, but a miserable medley of tribes."

IN 330 A.D. Constantine, first Christian emperor of Rome, consecrated a new capital in the east which came to be called Constantinople. Forty days and nights of tumultuous celebration followed, and rightly so. Constantine's city was to escape the doom awaiting the West. Horn-helmeted Goths would revel in the ruins of Rome while Constantinople reigned on for more than a millennium. In time its territories took the name of the ancient Greek colony by the Golden Horn: Byzantium. Greece itself stood among Byzantium's least prosperous—and most brutally milked—provinces.

Byzantine schoolboys studied the Attic dialect and read Homer and the old Athenian authors. The new Christian thinkers incorporated classical achievements in their own work, but only where they happened to fit. Theology had put philosophy in the shade. Athens itself was declining to the position of a college town. Provincial governors complained of its "pagan" professors and sullen students. As a result

WARRIORS of Greece throughout the centuries are shown in these drawings. To the left stand Fifth Century B.C. soldiers arrayed in leather kilts and bronze armor. At far left a messenger stands ready.

MONARCH commanding Byzantine soldiers around 1000 A.D. *(right)* wears a costume descended from Roman styles, with a metal-scaled cuirass, heavy stockings and knee-high boots decorated with pearls.

Athens' one remaining claim to fame, the Platonic Academy, was closed down in the year 529 by order of the Emperor Justinian. But this great ruler also ordered that his later additions to the Roman law be published not only in Latin but in Greek as well. By 620 even the Byzantine coinage was Greek-inscribed. Perforce the Greeks were learning to regard Constantinople and not Athens as their capital of letters and of law alike.

THOUGH Byzantium escaped the fate of Rome, its Greek provinces were often invaded during the next centuries. Goths, Vandals, Huns and Slavs raided various parts of the mainland, penetrating as far south as Corinth.

At the end of the 10th Century, Greece's northern border again developed an alarming sag. Under their Czar (for Caesar) Samuel, the Bulgarians were advancing into Thessalonica. These incursions went on for almost 20 years. Finally, in 1014, the Byzantine emperor, Basil II, rode to fight these persistent enemies. Basil captured 15,000 Bulgarian troops, cruelly blinded almost every man and sent them stumbling home to Samuel—who died of apoplexy. By then Basil himself was offering thanks to "Our Lady of Athens" at the ancient Parthenon, long since converted into a church. In order to commemorate his triumph, Basil gave the church two seemingly miraculous gifts: an oil lamp

which never ran dry and a golden dove which fluttered unceasingly above the altar.

The year 1204 saw the Fourth Crusade—a wolfish expedition led wildly astray—sack Constantinople and dismember the Byzantine empire. Venice had both perverted and banked the enterprise; it claimed and got most of maritime Greece as its reward. Much of the Greek mainland now was nominally ruled from Thessalonica by Boniface of Montferrat, who had been leader of the Crusade. A tough Venetian, the Marchese Guido Pallavicini, held Thermopylae. Guillaume de Champlitte and Geoffrey de Villehardouin, two knights from the Champagne district of France, took over most of the Peloponnesus. Thebes and Athens fell to a Burgundian, Othon de la Roche.

It seems that Othon's Franks melted down the famous gifts that Basil the Bulgar Slayer had dedicated at Athens. As *Roman* Catholics, they felt justified in cleaning out an Eastern Orthodox church. Nor did the city appeal to them. It was becoming a mud village of ignorant starvelings huddled in the midst of a surrealist perspective, a fantasy straight out of a painting by Giorgio de Chirico: miles of empty, coldly gleaming marble colonnades.

The Frankish robber barons and their descendants established no real connection with the conquered. It was loot and boot, hunt and joust; a brainless although far from blameless

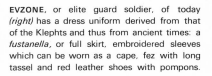

KLEPHT, or mountain fighter, who took part in the 19th Century War of Independence, is shown *(left)* in his red fez, elaborately embroidered jacket and *fustanella*, a white kilt. For dress occasions, as here, he wears highly decorated wool gaiters and square-toed shoes.

EVZONE, or elite guard soldier, of today *(right)* has a dress uniform derived from that of the Klephts and thus from ancient times: a *fustanella*, or full skirt, embroidered sleeves which can be worn as a cape, fez with long tassel and red leather shoes with pompons.

life. In the year 1305 an international tournament at Corinth pitted 12 great champions of western Europe against the flower of Greek-based chivalry. The home team battling order had a weirdly romantic ring: Phillippe de Savoie, Prince of Achaia; Nicholas de Saint-Omer, Lord of Thebes; the Duke of the Archipelago; the Count Palatine of Cephalonia; the Marquis of Boudonitza; the . . .

To do the dirty work in their habitual small wars, one of these lords imported a band of wandering cutthroats from the Catalan coast of Spain. Once hired, these stout fellows would not be fired. Some 7,000 of them formed a company determined to stay on in Greece. So, six years after the tournament at Corinth, the chivalry of Greece assembled once again. This time they had a stickier sport in view: chasing Catalans. The Franks got their quarry cornered, or so they thought, on the far side of a Boeotian bog. With pennants flying, the heavily armored knights charged halfway across the bog—and ignominiously sank.

THE Grand Company of Catalans had, so to speak, run up a smashing victory. For the moment, Greece belonged largely to them. New predators descended soon enough. Greece became a jigsaw puzzle of disunited princedoms: Frankish, Catalan, Navarrese, Venetian, Genoese and Florentine. Not only these, but

the Byzantines had won back some territories. And a strange new menace appeared on the horizon: the Ottoman Turks! The Greeks themselves were wretched altogether. Farmers neglected to sow crops, since others would reap them anyhow. Even bread became scarce.

At Mistra alone a few Byzantines managed to keep culture alive in Greece. The ramparts of this hill town were manned by painters, poets, scholars and philosophers while near-savages lived on the site of ancient Sparta in the valley below. The tiny court at Mistra was in fact doomed. And yet—as marvelous ruins still attest—Mistra kept a cheerfully creative spirit to the end. Byzantium's lost children lit a lovely votive candle on the altars of adversity.

The final fall of Constantinople to the Turks in 1453 brought a relatively stable although still far from happy era to Greece. Within a few decades most of the tormented peninsula would be folded into the Ottoman Turkish Empire. Of the European powers, only Venice kept some Greek holdings. The apparently eternal struggle between East and West had taken a new turn. As the western European states became more powerful and the Ottomans thrust northward, the field of contest shifted to the Danube Valley and to the high seas. Mainland Greece was no longer a battleground.

The Turks were capricious and occasionally unspeakable. However, they brought peace, freedom of religion, some tax reduction and a hands-off system of government which permitted self-rule at the village level. One of their harshest habits, which persisted until the 18th Century, was to seize one male child out of five for enrollment in the sultan's Janissary Corps. Frightful as this must have been for the parents, the boys themselves were well educated at the Sublime Porte. Their training thoroughly prepared them for state service. These Janissaries, fierce Moslems although Christian-born, grew up devoted to the Ottoman cause. As officers and administrators they served their turbaned sovereigns proudly and well.

TRADE, like bureaucratic routine, seemed a mean occupation to the Turks. Watching their Greek subjects busied about such things, the conquerors smiled scornfully. But while the Turks nibbled candy, romped among the cushions, sliced floating feathers with their scimitars or pulled at hookahs, the Greeks gradually built up a middle class and a reasonably prosperous business world. Greek trading vessels reopened communications with the rest of Europe. More and more Greek youths became sailors. The horizons of the subject race were widening again at last and dreams of independence began to form.

But the cause of independence was to suffer many setbacks before Greece at last became free. One such reverse followed the great naval battle of Lepanto, fought between a European Christian fleet and a vast Turkish armada in the straits of the Gulf of Corinth. On that terrible and sparkling fall day in 1571, some 33,000 Turks and their allies drowned and the Ottoman navy was virtually destroyed. Overjoyed by this smashing defeat of their rulers, and urged on by the European commander, Don John of Austria, the Greeks revolted. But Turkish power on land was not affected by the reverses at sea, and the Turks took pains to reassert their mastery by slaughtering thousands of Greek revolutionaries.

Toward the end of the 17th Century, Venice again made a stab at mainland Greece. Its forces took Athens for a time and besieged the Acropolis. The Parthenon still stood almost whole in those days. After serving as a church it had become a mosque. Now the Turks rolled their gunpowder barrels into the building for safekeeping . . . a German artilleryman employed by the Venetians lobbed a mortar shell through the roof . . . and ruin resulted.

Venice grew sickly and after 1715 lost all of its islands except those in the Ionian Sea. Hoping to gain access to the Mediterranean, and seeing a power vacuum on the peninsula, Catherine the Great of Russia instigated a second abortive Greek revolt. The Turks used brutal Albanian troops to smash it. The Turkish hold arthritically tightened.

But Greece was awakening. Patriot outlaws patrolled its remote mountains, capes and bays. The brigand "Klephts," as they were called, wanted more than freedom from oppressors. In the heroic tradition they conceived of freedom as a positive thing, a good in itself. The ballads which they sang by their campfires in the Greek night rang anew with this idea.

Meanwhile maritime Greece flourished. During the Napoleonic Wars, Greek privateers got rich by running the British blockade of southern French ports. Thus they gained invaluable experience in naval tactics. Between the semi-independent salt-water state of the shipowners on one hand, and the bristling Klepht hinterlands on the other, Ottoman control of Greece seemed very weak. It looked as if habit alone —the phthisic hand upon the emeralded pistol butt—kept the Turks in authority.

IN the year 1821, on the 25th day of March (still celebrated as Greek Independence Day), an Arcadian archbishop raised a new blue and white flag. The War of Independence was under way. Politically, Greece had tossed and turned for 2,200 years, incredibly enough. Nightmares, fevers and waking glimmers of destruction had mainly been its lot during all that time. Now Greece roused itself, courageous and renewed after all. But the new day that was dawning would not be gentle either.

The deserted town of Mistra clings to a hillside near Sparta. Once a Byzantine stronghold in Greece, it has many imposing ruins.

A New Infusion, Strange and Opulent

The long centuries of the Byzantine Empire left monuments wholly different from those of classical Greece, but no less magnificent. To Greek simplicity were added Roman engineering skill and eastern opulence. From the fusion of these elements sprang an ornate but glorious architecture—and frescoes and mosaics that have never been surpassed. If Greece itself was a political cipher at this time, its spirit survived, in a strange and wonderful metamorphosis.

ORNATE DOMES decorate the church of the monastery of Lavra, one of the 20 monasteries that cling to the rocky hills of the Mount Athos peninsula which juts some 40 miles into the Aegean Sea south of Macedonia.

FORTRESSLIKE WALLS enclose the Iveron monastery *(below)*, built in the 10th Century. Athos has been a monastic center of Eastern Orthodox Christianity for centuries, drawing contemplatives from many nations.

BLACK-ROBED MONK greets his cat from the balcony outside his cell at the monastery of Lavra. There are female cats on Athos, and hens, but no female of any other species has been allowed there for nearly 1,000 years.

FINE FRESCOES on a wall of the church of the Iveron monastery draw the attention of a monk. The monasteries are rich in frescoes, valuable icons and holy relics. The monks follow severe regimens of fasting and prayer.

Four slender minarets, relics of the centuries when the church was a Turkish mosque, shoot skyward at the corners of Hagia Sophia.

PORPHYRY COLUMNS frame the immense nave of the church *(below)*, which was begun on orders of Emperor Justinian in 532 A.D. A Moslem medallion hangs at right.

BYZANTINE CROSSES in Hagia Sophia *(opposite)* show Moslem overpainting which disguises their shape. The church's great mosaics have now largely been restored.

5

A New Nation

THE tragedy and passion engendered by the Greek War of Independence—a savage conflict that lasted from 1821 to 1829—were never so dramatically portrayed as in these lines by an anonymous balladeer describing the death of a rebel leader:

*For three hours he fought against eighteen
   thousand . . .
His gun was shattered . . .
Then his sword fell off at the handle
And Diakos fell into the hands of his enemies
   alive.
A thousand men went in front of him*

*And a thousand behind . . . (and they
   demanded)
"Will you turn Turk, change your faith,
Make obeisance in the mosque and leave the
   church?"
But Diakos answered . . . and spoke angrily:
"Go, you and your faith, you infidels, to
   destruction!
I was born a Greek and a Greek I will die!"
They took Diakos and impaled him.
They stood him upright and he mocked
   them. . . .
"Dogs, though you impale me it is but one
   Greek lost,*

*Odysseus is still well, and Captain Niketas,
And they will bring low Turkey and all your
government!"*

Like most wars, this one was a kind of paroxysm. Vengeance, greed, power hunger and simple blood lust played their part in it. Men with a taste for torturing their fellow creatures found much to do, and often they held the whip hand among Turks and Greeks alike. No volume could catalogue the heroism displayed, nor the horrors committed, during the struggle. Though the war was dark with confusion and pain, the issue, for the Greeks, was clear. Independence! That was their whole desire.

Martyred Diakos, the leader he calls Odysseus, Captain Niketas, Kolokotrones and their kind were brigand Klephts who united and came down from the mountains to drive the Turks from Greece. At the same time the merchant skippers of the Greek islands combined to harry Turkish ships. Armed with perhaps a dozen cannon and carrying no more than a hundred men apiece, the speedy Greek brigantines soon made a hornets' nest of the Aegean.

THE heroes of the islands were Papanikolis, Tombazis, Kanaris and other seafarers who perfected a deadly salt-water sport: "Fire-boating." They would take an expendable vessel, daub her insides with pitch and sulphur, cover her rigging with tar and cram her with gunpowder kegs. Then in the night they would appear from hiding and steer the ship down on the enemy. When she was near enough, the Greek crew would set a powder train alight on their explosive hulk, cast off in their longboat and escape, leaving the Turks nothing to fight but fire, explosions and then the hungry waves.

Thousands of miles away and much later in America, the novelist Herman Melville took note of this terrifying tactic. The doomed whaler *Pequod,* he wrote in *Moby Dick,* "drove on as if remorselessly commissioned to some vengeful deed. So the pitch and sulphur freighted brigs of the bold . . . Kanaris, issuing from their midnight harbors, with broad sheets of

flame for sails, bore down upon the Turkish frigates, and folded them in conflagrations."

Between 1821 and 1823 the insurgent forces almost succeeded in clearing Greece and Greek waters of the foe. Independence stood within their grasp. But since this had been their only goal, they did not know how to proceed beyond it. They failed to add self-discipline to freedom. Soon the merchant-admirals and robber-generals were quarreling among themselves. Civil strife, and then anarchy, resulted. So the Turks returned and, with Egyptian help, reconquered almost the whole of Greece.

A LARGE segment of the Greek rebel power was shut up in a lagoon town on the Aetolian coast, Missolonghi, and besieged by an immensely superior Turkish army. But Missolonghi stood fast for more than a year. There the English poet Lord Byron died, along with many another volunteer from abroad. In its hour of doom Missolonghi was bringing a new nation to birth.

A letter written by a Swiss volunteer named Meyer, and smuggled out through the siege lines, shows clearly enough what the defenders' spirit was like. "We are reduced to feed upon the most disgusting animals," wrote Meyer. "We are suffering horribly from hunger and thirst. . . . Sickness adds much to the calamities which overwhelm us. . . . More than a hundred thousand bombs and balls thrown by the enemy have destroyed our bastions and our houses. We have been terribly distressed by the cold, for we have suffered a great want of wood. Notwithstanding so many privations it is a . . . noble spectacle to witness the ardour and devotedness of the garrison. . . . I announce to you the resolution, sworn to before heaven . . . to bury ourselves . . . under the ruins of this city . . . I am proud to think the blood of a Swiss, of a child of William Tell, is about to mingle with that of the heroes of Greece."

When Missolonghi fell at last, its few remaining defenders set fire to the ammunition stores, deliberately blowing themselves and their attackers to pieces. The very mud of Missolonghi was kneaded thick, as later travelers would attest, with broken shells and human bones. But as so often happens in war, the Turkish triumph turned into its own opposite. The heroic defense of Missolonghi had aroused the sympathetic admiration of Europe. Consequently England, France and Russia together urged Turkey to back off and acknowledge some degree of Greek independence. The sultan scornfully said no. Thereupon an Anglo-French fleet steamed into Greek waters, bent upon "peaceful intimidation" of the Turks.

The Turkish navy was overconfident. Acting in concert with the Egyptian, it had long since turned the tables on the Greek island brigs and driven them into hiding. Moreover the Allied task force, although reinforced by Russian ships, had less than half the Moslem tonnage and armament. But the sea-dog sons of the Prophet overlooked the superior firepower of the West. In the Bay of Navarino, in October 1827, they challenged the Allied fleet. In the following four hours, no less than 60 ships went to the bottom—every one a Moslem vessel. The Turkish might had suddenly been swallowed up in the salt sea. Greek sovereignty was now assured, though this had not been done by Greece.

A CONFERENCE of the European allies resolved that Greece must become an independent state. They first imported an adolescent Bavarian prince named Otho. Proving unpopular and ineffectual, he was ultimately withdrawn. George, a prince of Denmark, finally ascended the throne, thus founding Greece's present royal family. George's many regal connections helped make Greece a part of the European community. He was an honorable and modest monarch, personally committed to constitutional government. George reigned both patiently and well for half a century, from 1863 to 1913. During all that time his little country grew in power and prosperity. By dint of rough but limited struggles with Turkey and the Balkan states, Greece even doubled its territory to the north and among the Aegean islands.

When George fell before an assassin's bullet, his proud son Constantine became king. The next year World War I began to shake all Europe. Constantine unfortunately had married a sister of the Kaiser. Antidemocratic and German-trained, he naturally favored the Kaiser's cause—as the Greek people did not.

King Constantine's prime minister, Eleutherios Venizelos, expressed the popular will in supporting the Allies. England, France and Russia, after all, had assisted at the birth of modern Greece. Venizelos was among the most persuasive statesmen in modern history, but the king was strong and wily too. Pulled opposite ways, the government fell apart. Between 1914 and 1918 Greece was divided, stitched up, betrayed, campaigned across and reduced to misery. The Allied victory at last spelled exile for Constantine and vindication for Venizelos. This extraordinary man, the only genius, perhaps, that modern Greece has yet produced, remains a saint to some historians and a calamity to others.

TWO ancient and recurring Greek dreams seemed especially significant to Venizelos. They guided all his own life and politics. The first was the dream of a frank and free democracy changing with the times—untrammeled, but also not secured by anything much in the way of American-style checks and balances. Pericles had held to that same heady but dangerous path. The second dream went back at least as far. It called for the political union of all Greeks everywhere. This gave rise to Venizelos' watchword: *Megali Idea*, the Great Idea.

At the beginning of the 1920s, one out of five Greeks still lived in Asia Minor under Turkish domination. This huge captive minority—descended mainly from the Byzantines—had been a part of Turkey ever since the Ottoman conquest. Venizelos burned to rescue it, and even to reassert Byzantine Greek "rights" to Constantinople. By one great speech after another he made the nation believe that these things would have to be. With Turkey defeated in World War I, Venizelos received permission in 1919 from the Allied powers to send occupying troops to Smyrna.

This militaristic move shocked the war-weary Greek people, who in late 1920 forced him from power and recalled King Constantine. The monarch, however, believed that retreat now would mean abandonment of the whole *Megali Idea*. Grandly outflanking Constantinople, he launched a tremendous, do-or-die invasion of the Turkish steppe.

Turkey's bold young dictator-to-be, Kemal Ataturk, let the invading army come on and on over the high and dry terrain. When the Greeks' supplies were exhausted, their communications cut, their horses dying, their infantry blistered and sick, Kemal attacked. The Greek troops ran for their lives—and lost them of course, being so far from home. Fifty thousand were killed, wounded or captured.

Overexcited by their own unexpected victory, the Turks went on killing. They fell upon the peaceful Greeks of Asia Minor who now

stood terrorized, whole villages succumbing to arson, rape and indiscriminate slaughter. Meanwhile, back in Athens, a badly scared government shrilly demanded—and obtained—Constantine's abdication (he died a few months later). The Greek commanding general and his chief political associates were ignominiously shot—purely for having disappointed the popular hopes. Venizelos had warned that these executions would disgust Europe, and so they did. The government now called upon him, of all people, to pick up the pieces of his own shattered dream.

Venizelos sighed, and sat down in neutral Switzerland with Turkish emissaries. After many months he succeeded in negotiating a vast, lopsided exchange of populations: 400,000 Turks in Greece for a million and a quarter Greeks in Turkey. This was a terrible arrangement from the economic standpoint. The immigrating Greeks forfeited immense ancestral holdings in Asia Minor. In Greece they faced the prospect

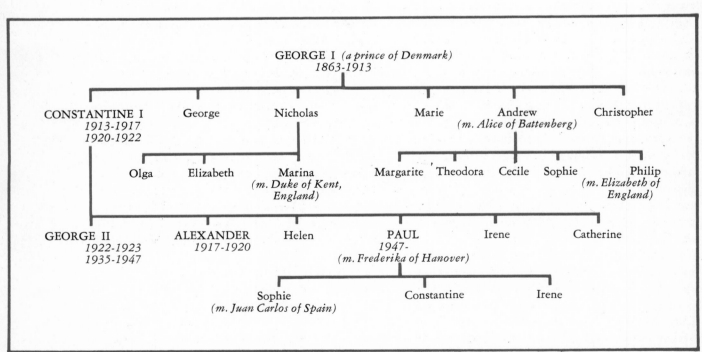

FAMILY TREE of Greece's royal house shows the line of succession which brought the present king, Paul, to the throne in 1947. Through marriages—like that of Paul's daughter Sophie to Spain's Juan Carlos in 1962—the family is related to most other European royalty. The dates indicate the years during which a monarch reigned.

of becoming beggars in effect, quartered on the already ill-fed and ill-sheltered native population. However, from the human point of view Venizelos had no choice but to push such an arrangement. The Greeks in Asia Minor still were being made to suffer terribly for what the Greeks at home had attempted. As immigrants they would be safe and free at least, and welcome as full citizens.

Actually the Asia Minor Greeks were resettled sooner and made their own way better than almost anyone had dared to hope. Their coming largely fulfilled, although in a rude waking way, the dream of the Great Idea. Cause for quarreling with Turkey was removed, and the two countries have since remained on friendly terms. Both are now NATO partners.

WITH his powers of persuasion and his popular support, Venizelos might now have become an uncrowned king. Instead he gave all his strength to his dream of implanting genuine democracy in Greece. He was high-voiced, feline, smiling and indefatigable in office. His private life offered little for enemies to attack; indeed he allowed himself few private moments. Venizelos' door stood open to voters and petitioners of all classes; only now and then would he go out into the country to pray alone at some mountain shrine. He must have felt despair at times, for the principles he taught were often misinterpreted as democratic license.

Venizelos failed to establish anything like moderation and fair play in Athenian politics. The forces of passion and of change kept plucking at his own trickful sleeve. He served as prime minister eight times—and suffered exile almost as often. Constantine and his son George II were on the throne intermittently during the whole time. Venizelos was in exile when he died in Paris in 1936. By then a new political rot—fascism—was spreading across Europe and Greece as well. General John Metaxas seized control at Athens in April 1936, sternly remodeling the nation along Axis lines.

The dictator even subjected Venizelos' body to the irony of a final "exile." It was to have been shipped to Athens to lie in state. Metaxas feared that the supreme persuader's presence—even in death—might cause a popular uprising. So he had the silent corpse shunted straight to Crete (the old liberal's birthplace) for quiet interment there. Meanwhile, following the Fascist fashion of the time, Metaxas vowed an end to all unseemly power struggles in Greece; also to political parties and elections.

This grim warrior took the trouble to ban a famous speech of Pericles as being "too democratic" for recitation in Greek schools. Yet for all that, the memory of Metaxas retains a certain aura in Greece. He instituted the eight-hour day, the minimum wage and workers' health insurance—on paper anyhow. He built roads and, most important, he modernized the army. And if Metaxas was fascistic, he was also a Greek patriot to the core. Early in the morning of October 28, 1940, the minister to Athens of Mussolini's Italy called at Metaxas' house. The general, in a bathrobe, answered the door himself. The Italian minister coldly presented a demand that the Greek-Albanian border be opened to Italian troops (who had recently occupied Albania). Metaxas said "*Ochi*," which means simply, "No." Within hours, crack Italian regiments were moving into Greece.

During the next few weeks Metaxas' army soundly and astonishingly drubbed the invaders, driving them far back into Albania. The spirit of Marathon and Salamis, it seemed, lived again. Mussolini's military pretenses had collapsed at once and forever. The conquerors of Libya and Ethiopia stood suddenly shamed before the world—thwarted by the skill and courage of a tiny but determined force. The Greeks still celebrate October 28 as Ochi Day.

THE next January, Metaxas fell ill and died. That spring German tanks, Stuka bombers and SS troops overran Greece. The nation became an Axis province: garrisoned, exploited, tormented, starved. But of all Hitler's sometime slave lands, none fought back harder than did Greece. The country had resisted foreign domination before, after all. Now once again the sons of the Klephts ranged the lonely coasts and mountains, killing Germans this time instead of Turks. By way of revenge, the Germans began mass executions. Tragically, the resistance forces themselves split into quarreling factions, and the position of Greece seemed as black as it had ever been in the past.

Two main forces were involved. One was the National Liberation Front (EAM), a broad coalition of liberals, Socialists and Communists which the Communists dominated because of their superior organizational talents; EAM's military arm was the National Popular Army of Liberation (ELAS). The other was the Greek Democratic League (EDES), a right-wing, pro-West and proroyalist group. It fell to Great Britain to attempt to resolve the dispute between these two factions, for wartime agreements with Soviet Russia had put Greece in Britain's sphere of influence while the rest of the Balkans was in Russia's. But the bitterness was more than the British could handle, and presently the evils of German occupation were compounded by the greater evils of an underground civil war. By 1944 the Germans, under severe pressure at home, ceased to play an important role in the struggle, and Greece was left to the two quarreling factions. The highly dramatic and dismaying upshot of this fratricide was that ELAS drove EDES straight into the Ionian Sea. The British navy rescued some right-wing guerrilla fighters, but ELAS had plainly won control. The Communists used their great moment for a fearsome purge of "collaborators"—meaning anyone not on the Communist side.

To halt the murdering and prevent consolidation of a Communist regime in Greece,

SUCCESS OF AN EXPERIMENT

The exchange of minorities between Greece and Turkey after World War I was one of the most extraordinary efforts ever made to ease international frictions. Some 400,000 Moslems moved to Turkey from Greece between 1923 and 1930; an estimated 1.25 million Turkish subjects of Greek extraction went in the opposite direction. Astonishingly, the exchange worked—in the main. The Moslems who moved were largely farmers; they were rapidly resettled in agricultural areas in Turkey. Many of the Greeks, however, were townsmen who were resettled as farmers. Others drifted to city slums. From these groups later came many Communist leaders during the Greek civil war. Yet in a generation most of the refugees had been assimilated into their new homeland. Today Macedonia is farmed largely by refugee descendants; Greek business has been enlivened by the skills learned in the Middle East by the immigrants from Turkey.

Britain's Prime Minister Winston Churchill firmly intervened. British troops were landed at Piraeus and commissioned to disarm the ELAS partisans. ELAS chose to fight for its weapons. Soon the British were firing upon the city they had come to liberate. The street fighting was vicious and intense. Churchill cabled the British commander: "Naturally ELAS will try to put women and children in the van where shooting may occur. . . . We have to hold and dominate Athens. . . . Without bloodshed if possible but also with bloodshed if necessary."

Continued bloodshed proved necessary—and in quantity—before "peaceful elections" were possible. And with the end of hostilities in Europe in the spring of 1945 came an ominous turn of events: Russia, which hitherto had tacitly approved the British efforts in Greece, now decided to intervene on the side of EAM, Josef Stalin hoping to convert the country into another Soviet satellite. When elections were eventually held in March 1946, the Communists stayed away from the polls. The Right Wing won a resounding but thoroughly suspect victory. General Napoleon Zervas, who had led EDES to defeat previously, was appointed minister of public order. At once he promised to "answer terrorism with terrorism ten times as strong, disaster with disaster ten times as strong, and slaughter ten times greater. And this is not anti-Christian, but God has taught us how to behave to anti-Christian Communists who sold their souls to the devil!"

Such extreme tactics helped drive the Red remnants into hiding in the mountains. The British, preoccupied with troubles at home, withdrew their material support from the Athens government. A regular Greek army came into being, but it showed small inclination to pursue the ELAS partisans. Before long the mountain villagers, with their long rebel heritage, came to accept Communist leadership in a new guerrilla war. They were hungry; they raided government stores and convoys. They were harassed; they replied with hit-and-run attacks all over Greece. Russian weapons, mainly smuggled across the Yugoslav border, gave the outlawed half of the population a chance of forcing its way to power. By the thousands, ferocious mountaineers swept down upon the lower valleys from the snowy ravines. Civil war brought the entire Greek economy to a standstill. The government did not know what to do. The Iron Curtain yawned like a guillotine.

Britain appealed to the United States. The need was urgent: if Greece were to become a Russian satellite, the western powers might as well concede the whole eastern Mediterranean. President Truman responded decisively. A U.S. economic mission was dispatched with all speed and temporarily given a major role in the Greek government. A military mission under General James Van Fleet helped reorganize the Greek army and supervised the forcible relocation of some 700,000 mountain villagers. With village support thus cut off, the rebels suffered terribly from hunger and cold. Now the reorganized army began to press them hard. Moreover, Marshal Tito of Yugoslavia, who was in the midst of his quarrel with Russia's Stalin, closed the Yugoslav border against them. Finally Stalin himself, seeing that the United States really meant business, quietly ceased to support the revolution. At that point the insurgents began burying their hand grenades and burning their insignia.

ABOVE the dying sputter of hostilities arose the age-old music of sheep bells and cockcrows. By the spring of 1949 the nation was virtually at peace. The question now was whether or not a reasonably free and democratic Greek state, given massive U.S. aid, could achieve some measure of economic health and earn the people's loyalty.

These things have since been accomplished. In the process, three main political groups have been struggling, under law, for leadership. The party of the Left, a Communist front organization, has had slight influence. The liberal Center, representing shopkeepers and skilled workers, has been vociferous but ineffectual. Oddly enough the pro-West Right, the rich man's party, has swept all before it time and again.

This continuing success of pomp and privilege in a country full of hungry, ragged individualists requires explanation. For one thing, the royal family, although frequently criticized for being too big a drain on the national budget, generally commands affection and respect. King Paul, Constantine's second son who has reigned since George II's death in 1947, is a gracious and tactful monarch. His queen, Frederika, is passionately charitable and almost irresistibly charming. Their prime minister, the black-browed Constantine Karamanlis, has shown surprising magnetism at the polls and velvet-glove firmness in office.

OUTSIDE the royal family, Greece has no hereditary aristocracy. The main criterion of social status, there as in America, is simply money. Moreover a high percentage of the rich are self-made. So a right-wing ballot cannot be construed as a vote for the dead hand of tradition. Rather, it expresses confidence in continued progress. And such confidence, so far, has not been misplaced. Many remote villages now are electrified. Some new industries have been developed, and tourist facilities have been vastly expanded. With the gradual cessation of American aid, Greece proves reasonably ready to support itself.

With each new year of peace the prospects for genuine prosperity also improve. But the Greeks are too realistic a people—and they have been through too much—to suppose that their age-old sticks and stones will soon turn into gold-knobbed bedsteads, cakes and candy canes. They hold up their heads, and once in a while they even go shopping. The land stays for them. It is still harsh, still heavenly.

In newly liberated Athens in 1944, British Prime Minister Winston Churchill meets with Greek leaders to try to form a government.

A Forceful Government Born of War

As German troops withdrew from the country toward the end of World War II, fighting tragically erupted again in Greece. Communist guerrillas in the northern mountains fell upon forces of the pro-western government.

Not until 1949, after a massive outlay of American aid, was Greece able to put down the rebellion. While the scars of war still show, Greece is at last politically stable under a respected monarch and a forceful government.

Besieged by Communist guerrillas in a northern village at the height of the war, government forces ready their guns for an attack.

CAPTURED REBELS are marched away after an unsuccessful raid in 1949 on a town near the Yugoslavian border. For a time, Yugoslavia supplied aid to the rebels.

CAREFULLY GUARDED, guerrillas are placed on trial for espionage in Thessaloniki in 1948. Many such prisoners were executed and others sent to concentration camps.

71

ACCEPTING A GIFT of the sword, scepter and crown of Otho I, first king of modern Greece, King Paul I *(center)* reads his thanks to Maximilian of Bavaria *(lower left)*, whose family received them on Otho's abdication in 1862. Prime Minister Constantine Karamanlis *(hands clasped)* stands at far left, Queen Frederika by the king.

and a restored constitutional monarchy

SANCTIFYING PARLIAMENT, Archbishop Chrysostomos *(right, center)*, head of the Greek Church, conducts a dedicatory ceremony at the start of the 1962 session.

CHATTING IN A CORRIDOR, politicians mingle *(right)* after the ceremony. Since 1956, parliament has been dominated by Karamanlis' National Radical Union.

ON THE COURTS of the exclusive Athens Tennis Club, Kostas Lyras, a director of Lyras Brothers, a leading Greek ship brokerage firm, races forward to make a shot.

AN EVENING PARTY for business friends is given *(right)* by Lyras and his wife *(second from right)* in his Athens apartment. He maintains another home in Switzerland.

A FAMILY GATHERING brings Lyras and his sister *(below)* to the villa of his mother *(far left)*. While a nurse knits, an older son watches a brother and sister dance.

Majestic bronze statue of Poseidon (or Zeus) radiates fierce strength and godlike nobility. It is considered the finest of the freestanding

figures typical of Greek sculpture between 480 and 450 B.C.

6

People
of
the Icon

"THOU shalt not make unto thee any graven
image. . . ." Simply by accepting that
prohibition, the Semites in general did much
to guide civilization in the direction of abstract
concepts, words on paper. The Greek way of
life was contrastingly sensuous and imbued
with art. If Jews and Moslems alike have been
"People of the Book," the Greeks have shown
a comparable devotion to the world of images.
The Greek word for image is icon, and histori-
cally the Greek race might well be called a
"People of the Icon." This too helped shape
what man has since become.

The most enduring images reflect that which
endures. Ephemeral emotion plays a part in
them but never the main role. Greek art at its
best was always self-sufficient, self-contained
and shaped to some ideal. Greek statuary remains unmoved and cool, like a stone in a
stream. The shadowy currents of emotion flowing over it may help to define the subject, but
they are not the main thing. The thing in itself

does more than evoke an emotional response; it awakens understanding, heart wisdom.

The literature of the Greeks abounds in visual terms. And their art was just as thoughtful as their thought was vivid. They knew how to put ideas in three dimensions. This power first appears among the Minoans of ancient Crete, whose small carvings have never been surpassed. The Greek image-making genius, dormant throughout the dark age following the Dorian invasions, reappears in the austere splendor of the so-called "archaic" style. During the Fifth Century B.C. it attains classical perfection. After the Peloponnesian War, in the Hellenistic period, it becomes yet more fruitful but less forceful. With the Christian art of Byzantium it flares into new life. Finally it inspires the Italian Renaissance.

TO begin at the beginning, consider the Minoan *Harvest Cup* at the Herakleion Museum in Crete. This modest object was carved of dark stone some 16 centuries before the time of Christ. Its subject is a ritual dance of harvesters prancing and joyfully singing, which encircles the cup. Here between the mothering earth and the fathering sun, brothers celebrate forever. Their work is done; the harvest in. Humanity dances in a ring, yet one's own hands can encircle it all. These harvesters, though stone, are as light and loud as birds. Here, in Simonides' phrase, is "silent poetry." And eternal thanksgiving as well.

Minoan art might easily fill a chapter in itself. The Boston Museum of Fine Arts has a monumental-seeming statuette of the Great Mother, with serpents in her hands. Her full breasts of ivory are bare, with golden nipples. This awesome nature goddess gives death and milk together. One finds her again on certain engraved gems, dancing, tiny and yet clear within the colored radiance. Such gems are far more than symbols; they display both an inner and an outer reality. Light-filled, they resemble ourselves in being both thought and thing.

The golden "Bull-Cups" found at Vaphio near Sparta and the inlaid hunting daggers of Mycenae carried Minoan style onto the Greek mainland. Homer's heroes drank from, and drew blood with, objects such as these. When their sons were overwhelmed by Dorian invaders from the north, luxury departed and art diminished to the geometric patterning of burial urns and household pottery. Then after some centuries the patterning gave way to pictures once again, and the Greek love of the human figure reasserted itself. A painted burial urn at Eleusis shows Odysseus and his companions putting out the Cyclops eye. Odysseus blinds the man-eater with a pointed stick, burning the single eye from the greedy monster's forehead. He will soon be stealing out from the cave with his companions. And this urn painting—which was itself rescued from an ancient tomb—symbolically expresses man's hope of overcoming mortality. Greek art in general, like the surviving pagan literature, is fraught with fugitive glimmers of this hope which Christianity made central.

As relative peace returned to Greece, temples rose on holy ground. These "houses of the gods," although patterned after the megaron, or column-supported hall of Mycenaean mansions, were supposed to resemble not real houses but ideal ones. Moreover, each one was distinguished by its particular relation to its natural setting. It would not be too much to say that for Greek sacred architecture, setting and perfection were what counted. At Delphi, Olympia, Bassae, Corinth and Sounion the remaining stone fragments and foundations bestow a kind of radiance on the surrounding earth and air. They still belong.

THE Greek temples were generally delicate and organic in feeling, yet abstract. Each one comprised a unity of related parts, like a beautiful body of thought. The Doric temple pattern, which multiplied all over Greece during the Sixth and Fifth Centuries B.C., is strict: a rectangular stone platform surrounded by steps and topped all around by a colonnade which in turn supports decorated friezes and a gabled roof. Inside: a walled room containing an image of the deity. Because their loveliest temples hew to this pattern, the Greeks have been accused of unimaginative and timid building. It was neither. The Doric temple again and again achieved an ideal. This ideal may be very different from our own architectural presumptions, but it stands. Indeed, it lives. Herman Melville put the thing in four precise lines:

> *Not magnitude, not lavishness*
> *But form, the site;*
> *Not innovating wilfulness*
> *But reverence for the archetype.*

What the archetype implied has been most succinctly stated by Professor Vincent Scully in his remarkable book on Greek sacred architecture called *The Earth, the Temple, and the Gods.* The Doric temple, he says, "cannot be viewed as a structural web, like a Japanese or, in a different way, a Gothic building; nor, on the other hand, as a solid mass, like an Egyptian or Mayan pyramid; nor, to go further, as a shell which encloses a space, like a Roman, Romanesque or Renaissance building. Instead, the temple interweaves [many] qualities . . . so that it can be seen purely as an articulated sculptural body . . . and the quality of appearing as a single body made up of many parts and therefore potentially active, would not have been possible if the Greeks had complicated the simple form. . . ."

The Greeks felt that their beloved land was marvelous enough for gods and men alike. The sacred places where their temples stood were as important to them as excellent architecture. Hence the essential modesty and tact of their temples. Chartres Cathedral has about the same width as the Parthenon, yet its nave is twice as high. Gothic reaching to heaven is just the opposite of Greek. Classical architecture balanced breadth against height, vertical columns against horizontal steps and eaves, to create open harmonies and work a glory without overtones. As a rule the People of the Icon were not mystics; they liked things clear.

Archaic Greek sculpture complemented the early temples. The stir of new freedom and artistic daring may be found in the life-sized stone "standing youths" of the Seventh and Sixth centuries B.C. Although clearly inspired by Egyptian sculpture, they are springier, more tender and alive than similar works in Egypt. The bronze *Charioteer* at Delphi is a further development. It stands very still, but with a breathing stillness. Then comes the full freedom of the classical age. The *Zeus*, labeled *Poseidon* by the National Museum in Athens, is truly a great Cloud-Gatherer and Thunderbolt-Hurler. Invisible energy from the whole bright and dark sky seems to fill this most marvelous of all single statues.

For group sculpture of comparable power, one must go to Olympia. There the carvings preserved from the Temple of Zeus create a truly epic effect. The east gable commemorates Pelops' chariot race. The still finer west gable shows the wedding brawl which resulted when the centaurs tried to carry off the Lapith women. Although done in dumb stone dim ages past, this struggle still writhes and shrieks like olive trees torn by an eternal gale. Yet the god Apollo, at the center, is about to call a halt to the half-monstrous and half-human storm. The imminence of peace imparts a mighty tension. The desperate women will escape their rape; murder will cease.

AS an especially creative art scholar named Charles Seltman has remarked: "The Olympia Master . . . saw humanity transfigured by its destiny; he pierced beyond this heroic world to more awful shapes; like Aeschylus, he was a seer and a poet who thought not in abstractions but in vivid images . . . in the centre stands Apollo, one arm stretched out above the tumult, the embodiment of Greek faith, beyond all others sane."

One of the earliest meanings of the word icon was "statue." And as Democritus said long ago, "statues have no hearts." An icon is not an idol. Neither is it an imitation of nature. Aristotle called it that in the Fourth Century B.C., and his statements have caused endless confusion, right up to the present. This confusion is inherent, for instance, in the poet e. e. cummings' little dictum:

> *a pretty girl who naked is,*
> *is worth a million statues.*

As a case in point, how about the nude *Aphrodite* that Aristotle's famed contemporary, Praxiteles, carved for the island of Cnidus? King Nicomedes of Bithynia offered to pay Cnidus' entire taxes in exchange for that one statue. The impoverished but beauty-loving islanders turned him away. Pliny called the nude the best "of all images that ever were made." Holland's translation of Pliny goes on to say: "So exquisit and singular it was, that many a man hath embarked, taken sea, and sailed to Cnidus for no other purpose, but onely to see and behold it."

Are pretty girls so far to seek? No, but the ideal of tender beauty is indeed. Praxiteles succeeded in creating such an ideal. In this sense he gave actual and visible form to the love goddess. An ancient Greek epigram put the matter this way:

> *Aphrodite gazed down upon Cnidus, and said,*
> *"Where on earth did Praxiteles see me naked?"*

The Greeks lavished as much genius on fresco painting as they did on sculpture, but plaster walls will fall at last, and only a few minor traces of their murals remain. The most revered Greek painter of the classical age was Polygnotus, whom we know by report alone. Considering his own work priceless, Polygnotus used to give it away. By way of recompense both Athens and Delphi awarded him citizenship and all expenses. For the market place of Athens he painted an epic morning after—the morning after the sack of Troy. And for Delphi he pictured Odysseus' visit to Hades. Scenes crowded yet calm, immense and terrible flowed from his brush.

The best painters to come after Polygnotus were a pair of rivals: Zeuxis and Parrhasius. These two seem to have pushed the art way over to the side of naturalism. In those days regular competitions for painting were held at various Greek cities. It is said that during one such contest birds flocked to peck at a bowl of grapes painted by Zeuxis. The judges thereupon attempted to unveil Parrhasius' entry—which proved to have the veil painted on. Parrhasius won that match hands down. It seems he used to paint in rich attire, as Leonardo da Vinci, Van Dyck and Salvador Dali were to do in later times. His shoes had golden buckles and he wore a gold wreath on his head. Zeuxis too was a fancy dresser. He once turned up at the Olympic Games in a cloak like a prize fighter's with his name embroidered in large letters on the back. Both men were superbly arrogant, Parrhasius especially so. He may—who knows?—have actually deserved the epigram (or epitaph) he wrote about himself:

> *The utmost limits of the painter's skill*
> *I've set. Fault-finders always will*
> *Find fault, yet by this hand I still*
> *Repeat: No mortal can surpass my skill.*

Alexander the Great carried Greek culture at his lance tip all the way to India and back. Thereafter, for many centuries, it dominated the Middle East and Mediterranean shores. The mosaics of Delos, Pella and Antioch, the funerary portraits of Ptolemaic Egypt, the Pompeian frescoes, all were petals from a single rose—the overblown blossom of Greek art.

Macedonian and afterward Roman domination both made for warring extremes in the life of Greece: wealth and poverty, graciousness and cruelty, faithlessness and fanaticism, ugliness and beauty. Immense quantities of sculpture came into being in these contradictory times. As the chronicler of Rome's decline, Edward Gibbon, remarked, the inanimate population of some cities bids fair to exceed the animate. Purists might condemn the Louvre's *Winged Victory* for its softness, or Athens' *Jockey* for its cuteness; still we are lucky to possess such sunset glories from the pagan day. With the Vatican's baroque *Laocoön* and Naples' *Farnese Bull*, however, night begins to descend. Greek art will dawn again, and soon, but it will do so at Byzantium, the Rome of the East. Moreover it will now be mantled with a new light: Christianity.

Byzantine art flooded and ebbed for a thousand years, laden with gospel bindings in beaten gold, carved ivories, jeweled crystal reliquaries, gold-spun embroideries, medallions and illuminated manuscripts. It cast random gleams across dark Europe, gleams of the old Greek glory now fragmented and reborn. As in the haunting song from Shakespeare's *Tempest*, Greek image-making suffered a "sea change into something rich and strange."

The very skies were hardening and brightening, from blue to gold-leaf. Nudes fled as the saints came marching in. With jagged gestures martyrs in striped togas addressed the tugging wind. Here and there stood kings and queens as stiff as playing cards, their robes like scaffolds draped with weighted flags. Eyes were huge and staring; fingers skinny and pointing. Scarlet serpents twined through purple texts. The Great Mother wept and covered her breast with a cloak of stars. Pagan Hermes emerged as rainbow-winged Michael the Archangel. Even radiant Apollo passed behind a purple cloud to reappear as Christ the Shepherd.

The last outpouring by the People of the Icon resembled their earliest art, which had long been forgotten and lost. Unconsciously Byzantium echoed the cups and carvings of the first Greek sea empire, the Minoan. Here again the wine of oriental mysticism mingled with the cool springs of Hellenic clarity. Once again richness of workmanship and ritual pageantry prevailed.

Yet Byzantine church art and architecture were something new under the sun. The Byzantines perfected the best way to set a dome atop a cube. It meant filling the gaps between the upper corners of the cube and the base of the dome with "pendentives." The word stands for supports shaped like triangular sections of a hollow ball viewed from the inside. Four pendentives make a smooth transition from a cubic space up into a hemispheric one. This invention may sound rather dry in the telling but it gave extraordinary grace.

Another Byzantine development was to add four wings, equal in length, to the central cube. Thus the whole church formed what became known as a "Greek cross." Often the wings in turn would be rounded off with half domes, increasing still more the lightness of the general effect. Christianity had inspired in the East a bubbling, exuberant, extravagantly beautiful style of sacred architecture. Constantinople is said to have erected 500 churches in the new mode. Greece itself built thousands, but they

MUSIC: A FLOURISHING ART FORM VANISHED

To the ancient Greeks, music and poetry were synonymous terms both designated by the single Greek word, *mousikê*. Every youth learned firm melody, right harmony and true rhythm, and the symbolic *ethos*, or character, reserved for each. During the Pythian games at Delphi, contests were specially devoted to music. No banquet was complete without its bard, his lyre and his song *(left)*.

In Homer's day professional reciters spread the fame of brave Achilles. Later, the poetess Sappho accompanied her solo lyrics with melodies she composed for the *barbitos,* or low-pitched lyre.

But it was in the choral odes of Attic festival and drama that Greek music found its most stirring form. Here melody, poetry and dance, performed by a trained chorus, were accompanied by the oboe-like *aulos.* Although little ancient Greek music has survived, there remains inherent in the words of Pindar and Aeschylus that passion and control of which music is the sole sponsor.

were mostly tiny. Dozens of ancient Byzantine churches still survive. Daphni, near Athens, has one of the most beautiful. Others at Ravenna, Italy, bear marvelous testimony to Byzantium's frontier work during the Dark Ages in Europe.

The mother church of course was Hagia Sophia—Holy Wisdom—at Constantinople. Buildings as superb as this one make praise superfluous. The architectural historian Nicholaus Pevsner grants it "a magic scarcely ever surpassed." Fittingly enough the two greatest achievements of Greek architecture (perhaps of *any* architecture) both were dedicated to wisdom. The stones of Hagia Sophia and the Parthenon at Athens are ringing still with silent music, which is thought.

ARTISTS rushed to do justice to the new church interiors. They usually reserved the central dome for the face of Christ as if He were peering from the sky. The pendentives underneath the dome were often adorned with the four Evangelists, Matthew, Mark, Luke and John. Above the apse Mary appeared with the Child in her lap. Wherever possible, fresco was now supplanted with another technique perfected by Byzantine artists: glittering mosaics of colored glass or stone. Hagia Sophia has a mosaic of the Archangel Michael that is unutterably splendid.

Perhaps the greatest Byzantine fresco is the one recently found under coats of paint, whitewash and plaster at the little Church of our Savior, or the Chora Church, near Constantinople's outer wall. Painted by a now unknown but superb artist of the 14th Century, it shows Christ coming like a storm of crystalline light to seize Adam and Eve by the hands and draw them out of Hell. Chora stands in telling contrast to classical Olympia, with its high relief of Apollo coming to still a mortal struggle. These two masterpieces, taken together, make a wide and lofty pair of doors to the Greek world: pagan and Christian.

During the Eighth Century, control of the Byzantine church fell to iconoclasts—image

smashers. These proto-protestants were grimly determined to create yet another "People of the Book." They ordered great numbers of art objects destroyed. Yet hundreds of particularly beautiful and sacred images were smuggled to safety in the West, especially to southern Italy. These, and the unrepentant iconolaters, or icon lovers, who went with them, helped prepare the coming Italian Renaissance.

In the mid-Ninth Century these Byzantine iconoclasts lost half their battle. Sacred statues still were banned, as being too clearly in a class with the "graven images" that Jehovah had proscribed. But holy pictures were again admitted to Orthodox churches, where they blossomed as never before. The very word icon came to have the connotation it keeps today. No longer does it bring statues to mind, as in ancient times, but rather a portable picture of a holy subject.

Portable art of all sorts, the more sumptuous the better, now became a Byzantine business on the grandest conceivable scale. Constantinople was a tastemaker to the Middle Ages, a golden honeycomb of artisans. One dazzled Crusader, Robert of Clari, wrote that the city held within its walls two thirds of the world's wealth. This reputation naturally helped bring on the city's ruin. In the 13th Century, greedy Crusaders sacked Constantinople. In the 15th Century, Ottoman Turks captured it and set about pruning Byzantine culture back to the roots. It seemed to be the finish for Greek art as such.

YET out of Crete in the 16th Century came a traveler, Domenicos Theotocópoulos, whom Spain and the world still honor as El Greco—the Greek. In the cool pointed flames of his art, Hellenic heart wisdom shone again. Modern painting owes a lot to El Greco; so does the spiritual adventure of mankind.

The People of the Icon have given the world a torchlight procession of great artists stretching back almost 4,000 years, always illuminating and reflecting that which endures. Was El Greco the last of this procession? Who can tell?

Gold death mask, found at Mycenae in 1876, dates from about 1500 B.C. It was called the mask of Agamemnon by its discoverer.

Silent Harmonies That Defy the Ages

Vast quantities of Greek art have been lost, meeting varied forms of destruction by time or man down the long dark corridor of centuries. But enough is left to prove the Greeks astonishingly fertile and inventive artists, masters of stone and bronze, of clay and pigments. Most of all, it proves that they were masters at capturing the harmony and beauty of the human form, in motion and at rest, and at conveying the strength and dignity of the individual.

*SERENITY pervades
the great bronze statues
which combine a godlike
perfection of form
with tense, human energy*

CHARIOTEER who once drove a team of horses with the reins that remain in his hands *(left)* is one of the earliest surviving bronze statues in Greek art. Cast about 470 B.C., it seems stiff, though dignified and powerful.

BRONZE YOUTH, cast between 340 and 300 B.C., shows the fluid and graceful modeling achieved by later Greek sculptors *(opposite)*. Possibly the work of Praxiteles, it was discovered under water off Marathon in 1925.

PENSIVE VIRGIN holding a golden-robed Christ child shines from a wall in the nave of the Chora Church in Istanbul, a jewel box of great mosaics which are apparently the work of one master artist of the 14th Century.

ELONGATED FIGURES of the ancestors of Christ—Enos, Abel, Adam and Seth—adorn a fluted dome of the Chora Church. Byzantine mosaics were highly stylized to emphasize the spiritual quality of the holy figures portrayed.

87

PAINTING survives on occasional wall panels and on many gracefully modeled and vigorously painted Greek vases

CRETAN FRESCO preserves an amazing freshness of design and color despite its having been painted some 3,500 years ago *(left)*. Found in the palace of King Minos at Cnossos, it pictures a slender youth with long, curly hair, an elaborate loincloth and a silver-mounted belt, and with ornaments on his arms, neck and wrist.

SUPERB VASES, the work of hundreds of different painters, are among the glories of Greek art *(opposite)*. Early artists painted their figures in black against the red of the potter's clay *(top row, right)*, achieving bold designs which nevertheless lack detail. Both vases in the top row opposite date from about 520 B.C. Later painters left the figures red, which allowed them to add realistic details in black. The vases in the bottom row, both dating from about 450 B.C., show a youth leaving home and a busy battle scene involving Athenian warriors.

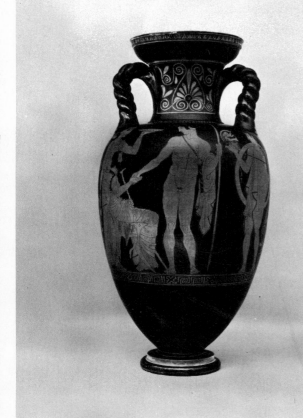

GREAT FRIEZE with hundreds of figures carved under the direction of Phidias adorned the Parthenon of Athens

SPIRITED HORSES dominate a three-foot-high slab, part of the Parthenon frieze removed from Athens by Lord Elgin and now in the British Museum. The whole frieze originally ran 524 feet around the building. Much of it depicted an Athenian throng, of which these horses and riders were a part, on its way to pay homage to Athena, patron deity both of the temple and of Athens. In other Parthenon reliefs, warriors fought battles famous in Greek history and myth.

DISCOVERY *of*

important works of art

goes on as scholars

unearth masterpieces

buried since ancient time

BRONZE APOLLO, dug up in Piraeus in 1959, is carefully restored by Greek archeologists *(left)*. It was probably buried in 86 B.C. when a warehouse where it was stored for shipment to Rome burned down.

FOUR STATUES from Piraeus lie on wooden beds *(opposite)* in Athens' National Museum. The first statue is possibly of Artemis, the next of Athena. The Apollo is next and another Artemis lies near the windows.

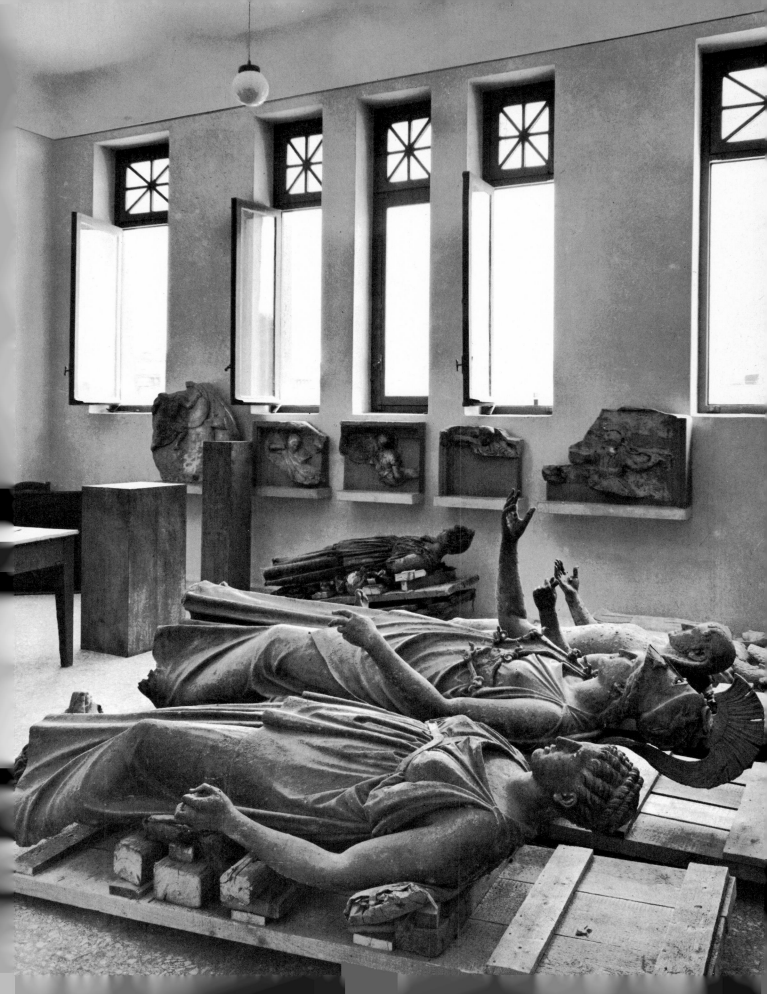

A packed audience listens as the chorus chants lines from a classical Greek tragedy during a drama festival at the theater at Epidaurus,

a wonderfully preserved open-air theater built about 350 B.C.

7
A
Sublime
Literature

ANCIENT Greek thought viewed in its towering entirety is like a tidal wave. The wine-dark hollow of the thing proves huge enough to cradle pagan courage, Platonic clarity and Christian compassion, all three. No survey will be adequate to such a subject. There is nothing for it but to plunge in and let the wave carry one from Homer's time along the rolling centuries, with dozens of authors briefly glimpsed on either hand.

Had the ancient Greeks been a "People of the Book," the *Iliad* and *Odyssey* would have been their Old and New Testaments. But they chose not to revere Homer as a prophet of revealed religion. Instead he was simply their best poet. The early Greeks made no distinction between ethics and esthetics. In other words they felt that what was beautiful must also be right and true. So they trusted in the beauty of Homer's songs. If Homer's poems did not have the authority of a bible, Achilles, Odysseus and Homer's other heroic figures still remained living examples to the Greeks for centuries.

Homer really did exist, it now appears, despite the doubts of many 19th Century scholars. The present consensus is that a poet named Homer composed at least the *Iliad* and probably the *Odyssey* as well. This blind bard lifted up his voice sometime during the Eighth Century B.C. Never since has he fallen silent.

HOMER'S *Iliad* is an epic tragedy. It tells, as Homer announces in the first lines, of the "ruinous wrath" of Achilles. Insulted by Agamemnon, the leader of the Argive forces before besieged Troy, Achilles sulks in his tent through most of the poem. He is the best warrior among the Argive leaders. Without him the other Argive heroes—Odysseus, Ajax, Agamemnon, Menelaus—begin to fall back before the Trojan attack. The fighting becomes ever more desperate. The Argives have been battling, far from home, watching their comrades die, fearing death themselves, for nine long years. They cannot quit now; yet neither can they breach the Trojan walls.

The *Iliad* ends with the return to battle of Achilles and his killing of the noble and generous Trojan hero, Hector. Homer does not show us the sack of Troy, but this ultimate horror of war is implied in the violence of the battle scenes. A tightly woven tragedy, the *Iliad* is generally thought the noblest and most convincing war poem ever written.

The *Odyssey* is a very different sort of poem. The war at Troy is over and now the hero is not thin-lipped Achilles but wily Odysseus. It is Odysseus' fate to wander for 10 years before he succeeds in reaching his native Ithaca. Accidents, storms and bloody encounters with monsters delay him, sinking his ships and killing the followers he is trying to lead home from Troy. No sooner has he escaped from the one-eyed Cyclops than most of his men fall prey to the cannibal Laestrygones. He must resist the enchantress Circe, who turns men into swine, and the entrancing Sirens' songs. He navigates by such nautical perils as the Wandering Rocks and Scylla and Charybdis. Finally, stripped of men and ships, Odysseus reaches Ithaca.

But his trials are not over, for he finds his wife, Penelope, besieged by suitors who believe Odysseus dead and want to despoil his fine flocks, fields and house. Disguised and aided by his son Telemachus and two faithful servants, Odysseus enters his palace and then defeats the suitors in a pitched battle, reclaiming his wife and kingdom. It is a triumph partly of brawn and sheer physical courage, but much more of intelligence and perseverance. Odysseus always finds a device to escape each peril; he is never dismayed. By extension, the *Odyssey* is an epic of every man's life. Every man is a wanderer, facing a succession of perils to his well-being and sanity, if not very frequently to his life, and using his wits and courage to get around them.

The *Odyssey*, like the *Iliad*, teaches *aretê*, a striving after excellence. But in the *Iliad* the emphasis was on courage in battle and warlike skills. In the *Odyssey*, however, Homer broadened the ideal to mean the generous bloom of perfection in life—not just the straight edge of it in strife.

THE epic heroes of previous cultures had been superhuman. For example, Gilgamesh (the ancient Babylonian equivalent of Odysseus) was celebrated as "he who saw everything to the ends of the land, who all things experienced, pondered all." Homer could have been aware of this epic. He introduces Odysseus in similar style, as one who "saw the towns of many men and got to know their way of thinking." But the slight change in wording makes a world of difference. Gilgamesh remains inaccessible, a myth. Odysseus, however, is a human being: desire-driven, storm-wracked, yet observant and resourceful to the end; a clever frontiersman of the possible.

Because of his unsettling cleverness, Odysseus has remained the subject of moralistic dispute all down the ages. The most dynamic men of legend "cheat" sometimes. Far from seeming "clean-cut," they appear in the round; they have their shadow sides. The German hero Tyl Eulenspiegel, the wily Plains Indian Coyote and even the Old Testament Jacob were sharp fellows too.

Smooth Jacob must outsmart hairy Esau in the nature of things. Jacob represents a new civilization on the way. So does Odysseus and this is why he too must conquer. Homer saw this, and by the power of song alone he gave the Greeks a new man, a new ideal, and drew Greek culture on. Why does the goddess of wisdom stand by Odysseus and help him to win through? In one of the lightest and most touching interviews ever held between mortal and immortal, the goddess herself gives the answer. "You are so civilized," Athena tells Odysseus, "so intuitive, so self-possessed."

WHATEVER seemed most valuable in Homer, the Greeks sought to preserve and adapt to their ever-changing culture. One such value was adaptability itself. One of Homer's epithets for Odysseus was "the man of many turns." Odysseus' emblem, a later poet relates, was a dolphin. This creature hemstitches sea and air on its exuberant way, moving from light into darkness and back again. Odysseus' own journeyings were similar. By indirections he would find directions out. Such was the Odyssean philosophy of life.

Aretê, then, is only half of Homer's legacy to Greek culture; the clear half. The darker part, equally needful in the human adventure, means to proceed through the unknown, mingling precision with suppleness. This intuitive side of the Greek way has received little mention until recent years. Being so caught up in facts and reason ourselves, we do not always recognize the less definable forces. Odysseus, however, set his sails to the undefinable. Bearings he might lose; awareness never.

"Homer," says Dio Chrysostom, an early Christian Father, "praised almost everything— animals and plants, water and earth, weapons and horses. He passed over nothing without somehow honoring and glorifying it. Even the one man whom he abused, Thersites, he called

a clear-voiced speaker." This genial custom was suspended by the next Greek poet: Hesiod, a dour singer. He was a shepherd boy upon Mount Helicon when the Muses first appeared to him. Hesiod himself avers, with apparent conviction, that the Muses commanded him to sing "true things" about nature, gods and men. One truth he made no bones about was that his own era—toward the end of the Eighth Century B.C.—was rough and hard: an "Age of Iron." Hesiod's *Works and Days* and *Theogony* shape mythology, folk wisdom and harsh home truths to the lofty patterning of Homeric verse. They are like a tart wine of the country served in a silver chalice.

During the next three centuries the Greeks invented almost all the forms of poetry that remain. Among these was the lyric: meaning simply songs to be accompanied on a lyre. It would be easy to list the lyric poets of ancient Greece, but unhelpful. In many instances their songs are all but lost. Sometimes a few lines remain: a single blossoming, miraculously dewy still, fresh music from beyond the seas of time. To give just one example, Sappho of Lesbos (as translated by Dante Gabriel Rossetti) sang that a particular young bride was

> *Like the sweet apple which reddens upon*
> *the topmost bough,*
> *A-top on the topmost twig,—which the*
> *pluckers forgot somehow,—*
> *Forgot it not, nay, but got it not, for none*
> *could get it till now.*

Other major forms, each appropriate for its own kind of thought, were the epigram, the ode and verse drama. Epigrams were meant to be inscribed upon stone monuments; odes to be sung at sacred festivals; comedies to cleanse the mind of cant; tragedies to purge and exalt the heart. Comedy apparently took its rise from primitive orgiastic rites. As for tragedy, it is said that the earliest tragic dramas replaced the ritual killing of Hellenic kings.

The great early writer of the choral ode, never to be surpassed, was Pindar. The founding father of the epigram was Simonides, a sage revered in his own day as a sort of Robert Frost. It so happens that both of these poets witnessed the epic defeats of Xerxes' invading Persian hosts. Naturally they celebrated these events, each in his own chosen form. Simonides composed the famous tight-reined epitaph on the Spartans from Lacedaemon who had defended Thermopylae to the death:

> Tell them in Lacedaemon, passer-by,
> That here obedient to their word we lie.

Pindar put his thanksgiving to the flute and the sound of dancers' feet stamping an asymmetrical beat. He honored God first and the Greek navy second when he sang (in Richmond Lattimore's translation) of

> Salamis, in God's rain and the bloody
>   death-sleet,
> where numberless men went down.
> Nevertheless, drench arrogance in silence.
> Not all the things Zeus gives are of one
>   kind,
> and Zeus is master of all. But as the
>   loveliness
> of honey are the honors that greet such
>   glad victories.

Aeschylus, the founder of Greek drama as we know it, also saw the struggle against Persia. Although he himself had fought the Persians hand to hand at Marathon he retained a profound human sympathy for his foes. He even made Xerxes the hero of a tragedy, *The Persians*. A typically sweeping, stinging stanza (translated by G. M. Cookson) tells of Xerxes' former slaves:

> They pay no more tribute; they bow them
>   no more!
> The word of power is not spoken
> By the Princes of Persia; their day is o'er,
> And the laws of the Medes are broken
> Through Asia's myriad-peopled land;
> For the staff is snapped in the King's right
>   hand.

Aeschylus' greatest surviving plays, the trilogy called the *Oresteia*, return to the world of the *Iliad*. They tell of Agamemnon's homecoming from Troy, his murder by his wife, Clytemnestra, and her death at the revenging hand of their son, Orestes. In the third play of the trilogy, Orestes is pursued by demonic furies. He flees to Athens, is tried for matricide and with divine aid wins an acquittal. Aeschylus is plainly giving thanks that the days of blood justice, of an eye for an eye, had passed. He celebrates the law of reason and reverence combined.

SOPHOCLES, who was born a generation after Aeschylus, wrote less resounding and magnificent poetry, but he was the more expert dramatist. His *Oedipus Rex* is considered the most perfectly constructed of all Greek tragedies. Sophocles' great theme in *Oedipus*, as in most of his plays, was, broadly speaking, harmony. A man out of harmony with himself, with nature or with the gods was doomed to a tragic end. And he perceived that good men fired with pride and zeal to serve truth and justice could be most tragically in defiance of these harmonies.

Euripides too shows the effects of pride, but even more of passion. In his *Medea* and *Hippolytus* the heroines kill with lustful fury what they love best. Tragedy for Euripides is personal as never before.

All three tragedians wrote comic interludes too, but of their so-called "satyr-plays" not much survives. The comic heritage of ancient Greece consists mainly in the beautiful, bawdy and brilliant satires of Aristophanes.

With the passing of the golden age, literature took a speculative turn. After the collapse of Athens in the Peloponnesian War, the *polis*, the city-state, no longer commanded utter loyalty. The same can be said for Greek religion. The Greek pantheon was fast freezing into a mere set of symbols. Attacks upon the gods were thought to be in poor taste; so weak had heaven become. As for science: having raised some lofty towers of speculation, it shut itself up within them.

The new Greek, tasteful, intelligent, quick, brave and curious as ever, found himself rather at a loss. He had forfeited the sense of adventure, and with it Odyssean awareness. The sense of values, too, had fled his heart. It needed reestablishing upon another level, in the mind. And this was done, when all seemed lost, by philosophy.

Where Socrates had dared to question the old beliefs, his disciple Plato now perfected new ones. Plato held (as Werner Jaeger says in his monumental study, *Paideia*) that the wise man "recreates, on a spiritual plane, a quality of the mythical heroes of old . . . the hero's power to 'make his hands keep his head' against enemies, monsters and dangers of all kinds, and to come out victorious." Of course the greatest dangers to heroes of the spirit are passion and ignorance. Plato suggested Socratic self-control and closely reasoned Socratic argument as the best weapons to use against these. He condemned poetry as being vague, untrue and uncontrolled, though he himself had been a poet in his youth. The fact is that poetic and dramatic genius contribute just as much as logic does to make Plato's prose *Dialogues* immortal.

An outstanding modern Platonist, Huntington Cairns, states that "many strands are interwoven in the dialogues but always at the center as their meaning is the Greek insight that Reason, the *Logos*, is nature steering all things from within. In this approach, nature is neither supernatural nor material; it is an organic whole, and man is not outside nature but within it. By concentration on this point of view and its implications Greek thought and art achieved a clarity never equaled elsewhere and Plato became its supreme spokesman."

YET often while reading Plato's dialogues one glimpses a heaven reserved for heroic minds, a fair harbor beyond our farthest seas. Such is the world of Ideas, eternal, immutable and perfectly beautiful, which Plato considered the true reality. We see but shadows, he insisted. In the *Symposium* (as translated by Michael Joyce) Plato puts a most alluring question:

"But if it were given to man to gaze on beauty's very self—unsullied, unalloyed and freed

THE FOUR GREAT GREEK DRAMATISTS

The Greeks of the classical age considered Aeschylus, Sophocles, Euripides and Aristophanes their four greatest playwrights. There were other dramatists but, less admired, their plays were less frequently copied by scribes and have all but vanished. Even the work of the four major dramatists is tragically incomplete. Sophocles, for example, is said to have written 123 plays; only seven have been preserved. We have, in all, 44 plays by the four men. They are conceded to be the world's finest body of dramatic literature.

AESCHYLUS was the first of the great dramatists. The immediate precursors of his plays were odes sung or chanted in unison by a chorus, and his seven surviving dramas show the influence of these odes. In the *Agamemnon*, for example, the chorus still has about half the lines, the characters the other half. This suited Aeschylus because he was a master of long, ringing choric passages and because he was more interested in probing, through the chorus, the social and moral significance of what his characters did than in showing these characters in action. He was, however, the first to bring a second speaking character on stage so that dialogue was possible.

SOPHOCLES added a third speaking part and created action and dialogue that pointed their own moral. His most forceful weapon was the kind of irony that results when the audience knows a truth about a character of which the character is ignorant. In *Oedipus Rex* the audience knows that Oedipus is guilty of killing his father and marrying his mother. Through a series of outrageous accidents, Oedipus has done just that, but he does not know it. In most of his speeches, however, Oedipus inadvertently says something which points to the fearful truth he cannot see. As a result, Sophocles sets up an excruciating tension as the audience, constantly reminded of the truth, awaits the catastrophe. Irony also served to express one of Sophocles' recurring themes: that man is blind and cannot perceive the truth about himself.

EURIPIDES' plays are bloodbursts of passion gone wild. If Aeschylus wrote, generally speaking, of the nature of justice in the community, and Sophocles of the "blind" man's violation of a universal order, Euripides wrote of the individual in the throes of a mania which has little relation to his community, or to nature. In *Medea* the heroine, having been deserted by her husband, Jason, murders her two children and Jason's new wife in her jealous rage. The play seems to have significance solely in its presentation of Medea and her passion. In short, Euripides' plays approach psychological drama—couched in magnificent poetry.

ARISTOPHANES was the most admired comic playwright of his times. His plays combine hilarious "low" comedy (with plenty of slapstick), graceful lyric passages and sharp satire. Presented after the tragedies during Athens' drama festivals, they were far from being merely comic relief, for they savagely lashed what Aristophanes considered the follies of his countrymen. They were, however, the perfect complement to the tragedies: they showed man not nobly tragic but grotesquely funny—cowardly, lecherous, greedy and absurd.

from the mortal taint that haunts the frailer loveliness of flesh and blood—if, I say, it were given to man to see the heavenly beauty face to face, would you call *his* . . . an unenviable life, whose eyes had been opened to the vision, and who had gazed upon it in true contemplation until it had become his own forever?

"And remember . . . that it is when he looks upon beauty's visible presentment, and only then, that a man will be quickened with the true, and not the seeming, virtue. . . . He shall be called the friend of god, and if ever it is given a man to put on immortality, it shall be given to him."

THE two greatest philosophers in history were but a generation apart, and one taught the other. Aristotle, the younger man, spent no less than 20 years at Plato's Athenian Academy, from 367 to 347. Like many subsequent philosophers, Aristotle was not so confident as Plato that dialectical argument will yield immutable ideal concepts. He concerned himself more with observed facts. All philosophy since has tended either toward Plato's idealism or Aristotle's practicality.

Aristotle himself undertook to set a course for a comet, or in other words to educate King Philip's boy, the Macedonian prince Alexander. Aristotle described the ideal hero as one who "would prefer short intense pleasures to long quiet ones; would choose to live nobly for a year rather than to pass many years of ordinary life; would rather do one great and noble deed than many small ones." Alexander certainly was like that.

While the conqueror crashed away to the Indus, Aristotle himself settled down at his own school in Athens to enjoy the long quiet pleasures of contemplation, research and teaching. All we have from him now are lecture notes, rough reading but immensely rich. Aristotle used history to explain politics; cogently defended poetry against Plato's strictures; pushed metaphysics to the point of positing an "Unmoved Mover" in God's place; greatly refined logical method; and laid the foundations for a

renaissance of science. His ultimate counsel (like Plato's and indeed like Homer's) was to *seize the beautiful*, at the point where truth and beauty become one thing.

Later Greek philosophers found this increasingly difficult. So they bent their thoughts to more everyday problems of good and evil. Even those who accepted the classic doctrine that "evil is the absence of good" were hard put to keep such "absence" at a distance. The so-called Epicurean, Sceptic, Cynic and Stoic philosophies all came out of this struggle. All four were propounded at Athens. The city remained the "School of Hellas" and of burgeoning Rome as well, but in a sadly constricted sense. In Hellenistic times Athens had diminished to the condition of a university town, the Cambridge of the Caesars. Educated Romans made a practice of conversing in Greek, much as the 19th Century Russians used French. The cultural and intellectual magnificence of Rome, somewhat stiff and grim as it was, owed almost everything to twilight Athens.

ARISTOTLE had begun the practice of scientific classification and research; his disciples continued this on a grand scale. But while Athens retained its title as the philosophic capital, science and scholarship moved south to wealthy Alexandria upon the Nile Delta. Alexandria's "Museum," or Temple of the Muses, held hundreds of scholarly investigators and more than half a million papyrus scrolls. As a physician-in-residence named Erasistratus noted: "Those who are altogether unaccustomed to research are at the first exercise of their intelligence befogged and blinded and quickly desist owing to fatigue . . . like those who without training try to run a race. But one who is accustomed to investigation, worming his way through and turning in all directions, does not give up the search, I will not say day or night, but his whole life long."

Among those who lived or studied in Alexandria and did not give up the search: Euclid, who composed the *Elements of Geometry;* Ctesibus, who invented the water clock and the water organ; Archimedes, who constructed a planetarium and made a science of mechanics; Aristarchus of Samos, the first great Alexandrian astronomer, who suggested that the earth orbits around the sun; Galen, who described human anatomy down to the nerve ends; and Ptolemy, who mapped earth and heaven. Ptolemy was also a poet, as it happens. One of his epigrams still is fragrant with the freedom of profound intelligence. In Dudley Fitts's paraphrase it reads:

> That I am mortal I know and do confess
> My span of a day:
> but when I gaze upon
> The thousandfold circling gyre of the stars,
> No longer do I walk on earth
> but rise
> The peer of God himself to take my fill
> At the ambrosial banquet of the Undying.

Throughout the eastern half of the Roman Empire, Greek was the common tongue. This gave freedom of movement to ideas; also it produced an increasing awareness of the brotherhood of man. Typical in spirit and biography was the Greek poet Meleager: born in Syrian Gadara, raised in Phoenician Tyre, died in Aegean Cos. His epitaph, which he himself wrote within a generation of Jesus' birth, concludes:

> Now if thou are a Syrian, SALAAM,
> And if a Phoenician, NAIDIOS,
> And if a Greek, FARE-WELL
> And say thou the same.

Saint Paul carried the word of God to the gentiles—in Greek, naturally. Thereafter the Four Gospels were written down for the first time—again in Greek, except perhaps for Matthew. The Greek New Testament conquered the world for Christ. Did its language influence the actual content? The answer must be yes in some degree. Scholars have even used internal evidence to show that the Apostle Luke was a Greek himself. Moreover the Apostle John appears to have been influenced by Plato. Even so it would be inaccurate to call

the Gospels Greek. They mark the final development of Greek literature in antiquity, and at the same time they signal its effective end.

The actual end came imperceptibly. During the many centuries of Byzantine Christian rule, the clear Hellenic tide lapped, oozed and fell. Yet ancient Greece left imperishable word relics bleaching like the delicate wing bones of sea birds upon the shores of barbarous Europe. And these bones were to rise again.

Johannes Scotus, an Irish scholar, read the ancient Greeks in their own tongue. But this Dark Ages philosopher was an exception. Latin translations of Aristotle were the dominant force in medieval learning. The universities that blossomed with the coming of the Middle Ages—at Salerno, Bologna, Paris, Oxford, Cambridge, Salamanca and so on—all put a Latinized Aristotle at the center of the curriculum. Not until the 14th Century did the University of Florence found the first actual Greek professorship in the West. Its sponsor was none other than Boccaccio, the humanist scholar who is better known as a teller of risqué tales.

DURING the century that followed, Ottoman conquests drove thousands of Byzantine Greek intellectuals to safe harbor in Italy. The fall of Constantinople in 1453 was thus a major stimulus to the·Italian Renaissance. Venice, the natural port of entry from the east, soon had a Greek academy and various Greek publishing houses. A guiding light of Greek studies in Venice was the printer Aldus Manutius. By the time he died in 1515, Aldus had published practically all the major Greek authors of classical antiquity.

The Renaissance flowered as swiftly as the spring. In its April, so to speak, Lorenzo de' Medici was collecting Greek codices at any price. And by sunny May of the movement Pope Leo X was instituting a sort of Roman Easter Egg Hunt for classical statuary, under the painter Raphael's direction. Especially Hellenic was the mingling of intellectual with sensuous enthusiasm. The English poet Robert Browning distills the savor of the thing in a couple of lines:

A Sublime Literature

Horses for ye, and brown Greek manuscripts,
And mistresses with great smooth marbly limbs.

As the Renaissance spread northward to England, Chaucer told again in *Troilus and Criseyde* a story of legendary Troy. At Montpellier in France, ribald Rabelais gave lectures on Galen and Hippocrates. In the next century, the 17th, Milton modeled his *Samson Agonistes* on Aeschylus' *Prometheus Bound*. Ben Jonson, too, derived his poetic art from Hellenic prototypes. He could take a single obsidian line, such as Lucian of Samosata's *All things pass by us, or we pass by them,* and reply in pure Greek spirit:

It is not growing like a tree
In bulk, doth make man better be

. . . .

A lily of a day
Is fairer far in May,
Although it fall and die that night
It was the plant and flower of light.

The age of reason and revolution also joined hands with the classical Greeks. Alexander the Great had kept a copy of Homer by his bed. Thomas Jefferson chose Origen, the Alexandrian sage, for his own nighttime reading. The Constitution of the United States was shaped in accordance with ancient Greek models. It profited by Greek mistakes as well. James Madison took an invaluable hint from the tragic course of Athenian democracy after Pericles. To prevent something similar from happening in America, he advocated a system of orderly representation hedged with checks and balances. "In all very numerous assemblies," Madison noted, "passion never fails to wrest the sceptre from reason. Had every Athenian citizen been a Socrates, every Athenian assembly would still have been a mob."

The so-called romantics of the 19th Century were classicists too. Goethe devoted the second part of his lifework, *Faust,* to a symbolic love affair with Helen of Troy. Byron, Wordsworth, Coleridge, Keats and Shelley burned with Greek ideals and images. Tolstoy taught himself Greek at 42, and passed his new learning on to his children. "Without a knowledge of Greek," he concluded, "there is no education." America's Walt Whitman used to urge the Greek Muses to come away west. Meanwhile he loved riding up and down Broadway in a horsecar, sitting perched on the box beside the driver and declaiming Homer at the top of his voice. But strangely enough the most poignant American tribute to the Hellenic spirit was penned by that pale and wild alcoholic, Edgar Allan Poe:

Helen, thy beauty is to me
Like those Nicéan barks of yore,
That gently, o'er a perfumed sea,
The weary, way-worn wanderer bore
To his own native shore.

On desperate seas long wont to roam,
Thy hyacinth hair, thy classic face,
Thy Naiad airs have brought me home
To the glory that was Greece,
And the grandeur that was Rome.

The literary legacy of Greece remains an unfailing inspiration and guide. James Joyce's *Ulysses* and the French dramas of Jean Giraudoux, Jean Cocteau and Jean Anouilh attest as much. A modern historian of the classic tradition, Gilbert Highet, makes the point negatively: "Imagine that all the books, plays and poems, in all the European languages, which were written under direct inspiration from the classics, should be destroyed. Not only would nearly all the best work disappear—Dante's Comedy . . . much of the finest nineteenth-century poetry— but several complete areas of European literature would drop out of sight entirely, like cities swallowed up in an earthquake, leaving nothing behind but a few flowers growing on the edge of the chasm. . . ."

This awful fantasy might well be broadened to include most realms of culture. Medicine, mathematics, physics, politics, philosophy, even athletics—all these things as we know them were Greek-born. The Greek contribution to western civilization requires no praise. It has amounted, as the English philosopher John Stuart Mill wrote, to "the indispensable first steps, which are the foundation of all the rest."

Bright-faced children are amused during class at an elementary school in Athens. In most Greek schools classes are overcrowded.

Revitalizing the Nation's Cultural Life

After centuries of oppression, wars and revolutions the Greeks are reasserting their age-old drive to produce the creative intellect, the cultured, active citizen. The public school system is improving with an increased budget, new buildings and a recent reform of the outmoded curriculum. The universities and technical schools have growing enrollments. And in the film and the novel, as well as in older forms, Greek art is giving definite signs of new life.

103

A STUDENT follows a rigorous

plan of study at a school supported

by Americans and Greeks together

SPORTS PERIOD delights Demetrios Sioris, a 16-year-old student at Athens College, a private preparatory school founded in 1925 and headed by an American.

NIGHT STUDY occupies Demetrios after a long day at school. Like schools in America, Athens College combines humane and scientific studies, work and athletics.

SCHOOL BUS carries Demetrios *(center)* home from the school's campus in Psychico, an Athens suburb. Four fifths of the college's 1,200 students are day pupils.

LABORATORY WORK in biology engrosses Demetrios *(left)*. Many of Athens College's graduates have made significant contributions to Greek culture and science.

UNIVERSITIES are growing but cannot fill the nation's need for teachers and technicians

CROWDED DESKS fill the main reading room of the library *(left)* at Athens' National and Capodistrian University. Greece has one other major university: the Aristotelian, in Thessaloniki.

COMPOSER Manos Hadjidakis *(opposite)* attempts to revitalize Greek music by basing his compositions on folk themes. He has also written musical scores for films.

ACTRESS Melina Mercouri has won world notice for her film roles in *Never on Sunday, He Who Must Die* and *Phaedra*, but she is also admired for her work in plays.

GREETING THE DAWN, Isadora Duncan dances at the portal of the Parthenon in 1921. Miss Duncan, an American, often dressed in robes modeled on those of ancient Greece and did dances based on Greek classical art.

8

A Guest List

IF Greece is a new nation to its own people, for travelers it is an ancient dream. The guest of Greece steps into a realm that is half mythological, yet solid at the same time. He comes home to the beginnings of western civilization. Some of the pagan temples and even whole islands appear yellowed in the slow fires of the centuries. Yet each new day that dawns in Greece is as fresh and unsullied there as anywhere. The slow-sparkling Aegean seems to have been born anew with Aphrodite in the night. Somehow one's own thoughts, playing at will between past and present, find refreshment too. An astonishingly high proportion of the country's

visitors report that Greece has worked some dramatic change in their own minds. Why should this be so? The fact remains as difficult to explain as to deny. Instead of speculating uselessly, let us draw up a list of distinguished guests —to see how Greece changed them and how they affected Greece. The procession will be motley to say the least: looters, teachers, martyrs, lovers, diggers, a dancer, and poets first and last.

The modern list begins with two aristocratic children of the British Empire, the Lords Elgin and Byron. Greek history teachers still spit out the first name blackly and caress the second to a high degree of shine. While serving as ambassador to the Sublime Porte at Constantinople around 1800, Elgin got carte blanche from the Ottoman sultan, allowing him to pillage Athens of antiquities. He subsequently hired 400 workmen, put scaffolding around the Parthenon and systematically stripped away its best remaining sculpture, which he shipped to England. He also plucked a caryatid from the neighboring Erechtheum and scores of lesser marbles from scattered sites elsewhere in Greece. Elgin did all this to "protect" sculptures that had survived more than 22 centuries without him.

They now repose in the British Museum. Greece wants the marbles back—although not to restore them to the Acropolis. Present fashion agrees with Elgin that art should be confined to museums—displayed like cut flowers instead of being allowed its own life in the sites for which it was made. The continuing quarrel over the Elgin marbles is not an art quarrel; it concerns merely pride of possession, since museums everywhere are much the same.

The other aristocrat, Byron, found Greece in 1809, when he was 21. They fell in love at once, so to speak, commencing an affair of passion which was to culminate in the poet's early death. The very thought of Elgin made Byron boil. The maledictions that he heaped upon his countryman still glint with malice:

> *Noseless himself, he brings home noseless blocks,*
> *To show at once the ravages of time and pox.*

And, on another occasion:

> *'First on the head of him who did this deed*
> *My curse shall light,—on him and all his seed:*
> *Without one spark of intellectual fire,*
> *Be all the sons as senseless as the sire:*
> *If one with wit the parent brood disgrace,*
> *Believe him bastard of a brighter race.'*

According to Byron's sometime friend Leicester Stanhope, Greece was more than a beloved mistress to the poet; it was his muse as well. Byron confided to Stanhope, as reported in the latter's memoirs, that "he had no mastery over his own thoughts. In early youth he was no poet, nor was he now except when the fit was upon him, and he felt his mind agitated and feverish. These attacks, he continued, scarcely ever visited him anywhere but in Greece; there he felt himself exhilarated—metamorphosed into another person, and with another soul—in short, never had he, but in Greece, written one good line of poetry."

In Greece, good lines poured from Byron's pen, and interwoven with them were passages whose simple splendor only the death of the English language will dim. These stanzas embrace history, and future history as well. Upon visiting the battlefield where the Athenians had first faced down Persian tyranny, he wrote:

> *The mountains look on Marathon—*
> *And Marathon looks on the sea;*
> *And musing there an hour alone,*
> *I dream'd that Greece might still be free;*
> *For standing on the Persians' grave,*
> *I could not deem myself a slave.*

Later, in a darker mood, he returned to a most compelling motif—Greek freedom and how it might be earned:

> *When Grecian mothers shall give birth to men,*
> *Then may'st thou be restored, but not till then.*
> *A thousand years scarce serve to form a state;*
> *An hour may lay it in the dust . . .*

The Greeks of his own day, Byron said plainly, "suffer all the moral and physical ills that can afflict humanity. Their life is a struggle against truth; they are vicious in their own defense." Such being the case, he went so far as to guess that "The Greeks will never be independent: they will never be sovereigns as heretofore, and God forbid they ever should! But they may be subjects without being slaves. Our colonies are not independent, but they are free and industrious, and such may Greece be hereafter." Present custom is to gloss over these startling reservations on Byron's part. He did, after all, give his life for Greek independence.

On his 36th birthday Byron was in besieged Missolonghi, preparing for, and hungering for, battle. This was not to be granted him. Instead, fever would destroy the poet in a matter of months. He was writing these lines to himself:

Seek out—less often sought than found—
A soldier's grave, for thee the best;
Then look around, and choose thy ground,
And take thy rest.

The next year, 1825, a cool-eyed American who was younger than the century itself joined the Greek independence forces as an army surgeon. Soon Samuel Gridley Howe became chief surgeon to the Greek fleet. The ideals of America's own revolution burned strongly in Howe. He was a pragmatist as well, and this combination of qualities made the Yankee doctor invaluable to the Greek cause. "It is not for this generation that we fight," he said once. "They are sunk in trespasses . . . but their children may and will be better." Howe's *An Historical Sketch of the Greek Revolution* presents the closest, sharpest and yet fairest view of the struggle that one could wish to have. But his accounts of the time-honored atrocities committed on both sides and his uncompromising word portraits of the revolutionary leaders do not sit well with romanticizers of Greek history.

Howe described the almost-legendary hero Kolokotrones as "a huge clumsy figure . . . with a face strongly, but coarsely marked; indicating cunning, presumption, and dogged resolution; which are in fact, the chief attributes of his character. Enjoying a high reputation for courage, he seemed to think any demonstration of it unnecessary." The renowned Alexander Ypsilanti (for whom a town in Michigan came to be named) was "brave without enterprise; learned, without a knowledge of men; and vain without self confidence." Mavrocordato (who commanded at Missolonghi) "cannot be called cowardly, for he will resolutely put himself in situations that he knows to be dangerous; yet, when the danger actually arrives, he, in spite of himself, loses his coolness and presence of mind." As for the female "admiral" Bouboulina, who lives in song and story as a Greek Joan of Arc, Howe conceded that "she defied alike danger and shame; but she was old, and

ugly . . . and greedy; and as for her disinterestedness, she owned that her sole object . . . was to get her share of the expected plunder."

Besides doctoring and reporting, Howe built a hospital, founded an agricultural community of refugees and started a school. His lead in offering that kind of constructive help has since been followed by other American altruists. In 1831 John Henry Hill and his wife founded the first girls' school in Athens, which is still going strong. In 1904 the Reverend John Henry House opened the American Farm School near Thessaloniki (ancient Thessalonica). This agricultural college goes on helping to increase the yield of Greece's farmland. A group of Greeks and Americans together founded Athens College in 1925, under Homer Davis' direction. Actually a school for boys, the "college" hones a sizable share of the best Greek minds.

THESE projects—together with Pierce College and Anatolia College, founded respectively in 1875 and 1886 in Asia Minor but later moved to the Greek mainland—sprang from an American feeling for Greece that goes way beyond romance. A sense of the enduring beauty of the Greek world and of Greek work plays into it. Witness Samuel Gridley Howe's own quiet recollection of a morning in the Aegean.

"I was once going along the beach in the little island of Scopelus," he wrote, "and my attention was attracted to a long and beautifully shaped boat, nearly finished. I approached, and found only one man, squatting beside her on his heels, eating biscuit and olives. I asked him, where the builders were? 'I am,' replied he. . . . I looked round for his tools, but not seeing them, asked him where his scale and compasses were. The man stared; I found he did not know Gunter's scale, from a gridiron. . . . After he had finished his olives, wiped his mustachios, and crossed himself three times; he got up, examined his little red cross, and piece of garlic, which he had nailed on the bow of his boat, to keep off the devil . . . he resumed his tools . . . his principal instrument, and with which he could cut, plane, and mortise, was a long well tempered knife . . . I wondered where he got his ideas of beauty and proportion, or if he had ever heard of Phidias or Praxiteles."

One American genius to visit Greece was Herman Melville, who stopped over briefly on his way to the Holy Land in the winter of 1856-1857. Melville had already known both great success and crushing failure. *Moby Dick* —an immediate bust with critics and public in his day—was behind him. Long decades of practically unbroken silence (during which he was to support his family as a customs inspector) lay ahead. So Melville's Greek journal was written at a turning point in his life. His impressions are brief, slanting and slight in the main, yet the lightning of a great heart plays through them. No one who has climbed the Acropolis in winter, with the quarried marble breast of Mount Pentelikon looming up in the distance beyond, will fail to appreciate this scrawled note from Melville's hand: "Pentelicus covered at top with snow—looking down on its child, the Parthenon."

IF visitors have found much to marvel at among the Greeks, the reverse is also true. Take the case of William Gladstone, Queen Victoria's awesomely proper prime minister. In 1858-1859 *O Gladstonas* (The Gladstone), as the Greeks called him, was on an inspection trip on the Ionian island of Corfu, which at that time was still under British protection. His official business done, Gladstone departed for the larger world of London. Presumably he was pleased to go, but not in the enduring legend that the Greeks have woven about his name. This is an apocryphal story as told recently to the English traveler Patrick Leigh Fermor (and related in his book, *Mani*) by a village elder:

"Mrs. Gladstone wrote to [her husband] telling him to come home. There was no answer. She wrote again and again and still no answer. . . . So she caught a steamship in London and sailed to Corfu. And there in the public square, what did she find? Gladstone outside a café on a chair and he had his right arm crooked over the back of another chair,

and his left over the back of a third, and a fourth for his right leg and a fifth for his left. A string of beads hung from one hand and the mouthpiece of a narghilé [a water pipe] was in the other; but the narghilé was out. Why? Because Gladstone was asleep.

"His top hat was over his eyes and his mouth had fallen open; but between his teeth was a piece of Turkish delight—it was hanging out. [Mrs. Gladstone] had just come from London where it always rains, she still had a black umbrella in her hand. And she gave him a jab in the side with this umbrella . . . and Gladstone woke up with a start: '*Hé!* What's happening?' 'I'll tell you what's happening, husband,' Mrs. Gladstone said. 'You're for home.' And she took him off to London with her. He was a good man."

Other strong-minded women succeeded in establishing rather bizarre beachheads on Attic soil. First among them was the Duchesse de Plaisance, a divorced half-American bluestocking who came to Greece in 1829. She instructed the daughters of the revolutionary chieftains in French and conversation, meanwhile keeping her own daughter's embalmed corpse beside her in a glass casket. At a time when the countryside swarmed with ferocious brigands, the duchess settled in a villa upon Mount Pentelikon, far from town. Court wags unkindly suggested that she enjoyed molestation, but this was a canard. The duchess was tiny and emaciated, "nothing but breath," as one admirer declared. The villagers revered and defended their little duchess. She designed a flowing robe in imitation of ancient Greek statuettes, to wear the year round, and preached a religion of her own devising.

SHE had a boon companion, whom the same admirer described as "a marvelous picture of health and strength [with] great blue eyes as deep as the sea, and fine chestnut hair. Her teeth are those of the privileged English race, with a milky whiteness that only flourishes in English fog." Jane Digby was her maiden name. While drifting southeastward across the Continent this glowing creature had become in turn Lady Ellenborough, Baroness Venningen, "Ianthe" (mistress to King Ludwig of Bavaria) and Countess Spyridon Theotokis. Her continuing affairs raised Athenian temperatures; she was snubbed by the Court. So the capricious duchess took her up. The ladies both had quality of will; across their obvious differences of temperament they recognized, respected and enjoyed each other. But in time Jane sailed away to Syria. Nearing the age of 50, she married a Bedouin sheik and disappeared from view.

WARM-BOSOMED Jane Digby and the flowing-robed duchess both seemed to live again, their eccentricities united, in the fabled American dancer Isadora Duncan. Those who saw her on stage still speak wonderingly of the Elysian atmosphere that "Isadora" knew how to weave—creating by the mere motions of her limbs a free and timeless world. She visited Greece both before and after World War I, to sop up inspiration and to dispense the same. At dawn, Isadora and her companions used to wend their way up to the Acropolis, there to greet with dance the rising sun. More than a remarkable performer, she personally propagated with immense success her notions of pagan life and love. Yet, wonderfully gifted and giving though she was, she left a memory that also preserves a comic sheen; it appears as iridescent as a bubble of oil. Allan Ross Macdougall's biography of her, *Isadora*, tells how she first greeted Athenian reporters in a diaphanous neo-Greek gown, "And when they asked her if she didn't find some physical inconvenience thus dressed, or find the sacred marbles just a trifle too cold as she sat on them, she replied disdainfully: 'Cold! Who could be conscious of such things amid these surroundings? Did the ancient Greeks complain of being chilled when they witnessed the Olympian games? How can I feel cold when I am inhaling the same air as Phidias, as Pericles, as Alexander did, looking at the same scenes, inspired by the same ideas? Cold?'"

If Isadora steeped herself in a dream Greece, others came mantled in their own alien dreams. The most renowned, perhaps, was the British soldier-poet Rupert Brooke, who died on the way to the Gallipoli campaign of 1915-1916. For years he had envisioned being buried on one of the Greek isles, and in 1915 his ship stopped at the island of Skyros. Dying of blood poisoning, he was interred on Skyros with all honor, and commemorated by a marble youth called "Immortal Poetry"—whose nude condition displeases the island ladies. Brooke wrote his own insular epitaph:

> If I should die, think only this of me:
> There's some corner of a foreign field
> That is forever England. There shall be
> In that rich earth a richer dust concealed;
> A dust whom England bore. . . .

While Rupert was dying and Isadora was dancing, other enthusiasts had been digging. The archeological brigade includes some of Greece's most colorful and important guests. They were spearheaded by Heinrich Schliemann, the iron-willed progeny of a poor, drunken Mecklenburg parson. Schliemann early got out of Mecklenburg and set about making his boyhood dreams come true, especially in a business way. By the time he was 46 he had become a multimillionaire merchant, a master of eight languages, a classical scholar and a success in everything but marriage. His wife was a Russian shrew. In 1868 he made a visit to Greece, which changed everything. Schliemann abandoned business, divorced his wife and begged the Archbishop of Athens (an old acquaintance) to find him a new bride: "She should be poor," he wrote, "but well educated; she must be enthusiastic about Homer and about the rebirth of my beloved Greece. . . . She should be of the Greek type, with black hair and, if possible, beautiful. But my main requirement is a good and loving heart. . . ."

The archbishop soon produced the girl, a paragon at 16. Schliemann then confided to her the dearest dream of his life, which was to prove that Homer's 3,000-year-old *Iliad* was a work of fact, not fiction. The surest test, he thought, would be to dig for the long-vanished city of Troy in Asia Minor. Within a year the Schliemanns were doing just that. They hired 150 Turkish spademen to slice open the mound of Hissarlik, four miles inland from the Hellespont. Their choice of site accorded with Homer's descriptions, and it was exact. Schliemann unearthed no less than seven successive Troys, buried one atop the other. Among his finds was a fantastic treasury of gold crowns and ornaments, which Schliemann smuggled out to bedeck his beautiful bride. He called this trove "the Jewels of Helen."

Schliemann capped his first astonishing triumph with a second at Mycenae—Agamemnon's home on the Peloponnesus. The walls of this historic citadel were visible enough above the Argive plain, but appeared to contain nothing of interest. Schliemann dug a deep trench within the circuit of the walls—and found 19 ancient graves crammed with treasure. There were beautifully inlaid weapons of bronze, gold drinking cups such as Homer described, and golden masks on the faces of three warrior-kings' corpses. Lifting the masks, Schliemann

found that one of the kings "had been wonderfully preserved. . . . There was no vestige of hair, but both eyes were perfectly visible, also the mouth, which owing to the enormous weight that had pressed upon it, was wide open, and showed thirty-two beautiful teeth." Schliemann felt that the reigning king of Greece should be informed at once. He dispatched a telegram to the monarch with this inevitably controversial boast:

HAVE GAZED ON FACE OF AGAMEMNON STOP

The next great archeologist in Greece was myopic, romantic and willful—and the heir to a fortune. Coming to Greece in middle age in 1893, Sir Arthur Evans found it not altogether to his taste; classical art held no appeal for him. What did intrigue his eye were some small coins and engraved gems obtained from dealers and collectors and inscribed with an unknown alphabet. These he traced to the island of Crete, which Homer described as having had a hundred cities. Its capital in Homeric times had been Cnossos, near present-day Herakleion. Sir Arthur looked over the gently mounded and apparently virginal site where Cnossos was said to have stood. A vast olive grove now covered

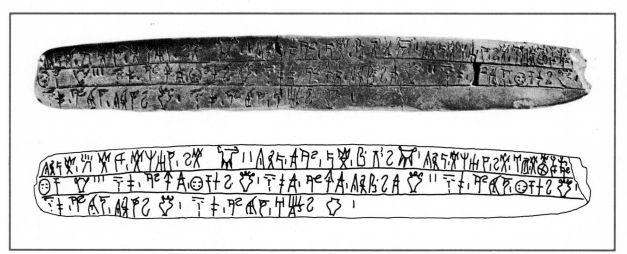

MOST IMPORTANT FIND of recent years in Greece was the so-called Tripod tablet, in the script known as Linear B. Uncovered at Pylos in 1953, the tablet *(top)* verified British linguist Michael Ventris' prediction that the script was an archaic form of Greek. Arguing from his study of 2,500 other tablets, Ventris had announced in 1952 that the classical (Fifth Century B.C.) Greek word *tripode* (meaning tripods) had developed from the Linear B (c. 1250 B.C.) word *ti-ri-po-de*. Conclusive proof was furnished when, on the Tripod tablet, each tripod ideogram (three-legged jars on top row of diagram) was accompanied by symbols for the syllables *ti-ri-po-de*.

DILIGENT WIFE washes the window *(opposite)* of her simple kitchen which has an old wood-burning stove. She is wearing the homespun woven by the women of Epirus.

SHEPHERD'S FAMILY whiles away the winter minding the baby and weaving as they wait for the shepherd to herd his sheep back from the lowland winter grazing lands.

SOLEMN SERVICE includes the placing of flower wreaths on the couple's heads by the bridegroom's godfather. The wreaths, blessed by the priest, are linked by a ribbon.

HAPPY DANCE follows the church ceremony. The relatives bring food, the dancing and singing continue until late at night and the men fire off pistols in celebration.

122

INDUSTRY remains limited

and few factories are automated,

but production is on the increase

LABORERS dump sacks of dried grapes *(above)* at a busy raisin factory on Crete. Raisins and other fruits are among Greece's leading exports.

A YOUNG WEAVER tends a loom *(opposite)* in one of Crete's larger textile factories. Like most Greek industries, this plant is privately owned.

FACTORY WORKERS take packaged raisins from a wrapping machine and box them for shipment. Many women now have jobs in Greek factories.

FASHION SHOW entertains some of the men and women
at a charity tea and card party in Athens' King George
Hotel. The model's costume has a stylish Parisian look.

QUIET GAME of cards in the hushed atmosphere of an
exclusive and formally furnished gentlemen's club in
Athens occupies five of Greece's more prominent citizens.

9

Shrine,
Church
and Temple

GREECE is not picturesque but sculptural. Clear light flowing over carved land and water, such is its essence. The colors are subtle, ever-changing, often pale. The crops are sparse, and forests few. Distances are not enormous; things within view seem all of a piece, and a man can walk or sail to what he sees. The human scale, ascetic tone and sculptural lilt very often combine to create a natural work of art as it were, from the hand of God. At the center of practically all such harmonies in Greece one finds a modern shrine or a Byzantine church or the ruins of an ancient temple—or even all three at once. It is generally supposed that these sites were "chosen" for esthetic reasons or for defense. But this is false. The fact is that the holy places of Greece always were revered, even before temples were built to mark them. They were sacred center points of horizon-wide natural glories.

Any attempt to separate the classic temples from the "view" misses both. The Greeks who first worshiped in these places were not romantic esthetes wistfully gazing upon an alien world; they stood within nature. Their temples, solid yet alive geometries in stone, affirmed the yet more living and more sacred architecture of place: of earth, air, fire and

129

water. The Biblical saying is especially apt: "In my father's house are many mansions."

The great pagan sanctuaries have undying resonance: Dodona, where Zeus spoke to his worshipers through the rustling of an oak; Delos, the floating island which was anchored in the sea after serving as a birthplace for the divine twins Apollo and Artemis; Delphi, the sun-washed shelf below Mount Parnassus from which Apollo's oracle counseled the whole classical world. Delphi was a kind of magnetic pole that not only attracted but also realigned the inner natures of pilgrim Greeks. They said it stood at the center of the world. Zeus himself had tested this by releasing two eagles from opposite ends of the earth. Flying steadily, the eagles met over Delphi. A pair of them soars there still, as thousands of modern visitors can testify. And Delphi still can be a life-changing experience for the traveler. Yet certain more out-of-the-way sanctuaries may give an even keener sense of sacredness.

ON the island of Aegina, there is a granite ridge from which one looks north and south across the water to Attica, Salamis, Troezen and the Peloponnesus. East and west are the gentle swellings of the island, rising to a climax in the sunset peak of Mount Oros. Just under the ridge itself, there is a round hollow cave, high enough to stand inside, from which one can see over the Saronic Gulf to purple Hymettus, the honey-giving mountain. Early Bronze Age relics show that the area was sacred long before the days when Ajax, from nearby Salamis, embarked with the Argives for Troy. There was a fresh spring welling from the rock of the cave, and when it ceased at last the islanders sank a well in the cave floor, very deep—it is there still. Directly above the well, there is an opening which leads through to the ridge top. By the opening above once stood a column with a winged sphinx upon it.

The summit holds the famous Doric temple of Athena-Aphaia, built about 500 B.C., which replaced an older temple dedicated to Aphaia alone. Aphaia was the local manifestation of the mother goddess. Athena, who partially replaced her, was of course the maiden goddess of wisdom—civilizing and severe. Athena rode the irresistible crest of human culture; Aphaia, by contrast, was peaceful by nature, unmoving yet ever renewed. One may sense the presence of them both in the cool feminine grace of the temple ruins, with the sun going molten down into the pale sea beyond the terrace, the songbirds slipping like clarinet notes among the columns, and the fragrant breeze rising through the pines from the herb gardens and pistachio groves down by the bay. It is possible to muse among the ruins for hours quite alone. Like listening to music, one tunes in and out of the experience as it flows on, a lullaby that says, "You're all right here for a while; just rest and see."

Anyone who stays very long at the temple of Athena-Aphaia comes to feel the pull of Mount Oros in the middle distance. It is a high sharp cone, barren, and golden in most lights. Sunrise shows a speck of what seems to be white fire at its tip. This is the chapel of Saint Elias, built near the ancient open-air altar of Zeus-Panhellenios—Zeus of all the Greeks. On this peak, as in so many Greek sacred places, a Christian saint has supplanted a pagan deity. Saint Elias took possession of Zeus's mountain shrines; he too became a weather-maker and a wielder of the lightning bolt. A cloud upon Mount Oros still is recognized as the first sign of welcome rains to come. And peasants all over Greece still invoke Elias to send sun and rain alike as needed.

SAINT ELIAS was a Fourth Century hermit, but Greek legend frequently confuses the saint with the Hebrew prophet Elijah, who ascended to heaven in "a chariot of fire." A monastery on the island of Lesbos contains a manuscript dialogue reading in part:

Epiphanios. *Do they speak truly who declare that the prophet Elias is in his chariot thundering and lightning among the clouds, and that he is pursuing a dragon?*

Andreas. *Far from it . . . but he has power over the rain, and can ask God that in time of drought he will give rain to the earth. . . . As to the fact that lightning burns a dragon, I have no doubts.*

At Eleusis, the ancient shrine of the corn goddess Demeter, A Christian saint, Dhimitra, came into being. Demeter's daughter Persephone was stolen away by the Hospitable Lord of the Underworld and kept hidden in darkness like seed corn for half the year. Persephone's annual return to life coincided with the springing up of the new year's crops. Saint Dhimitra's daughter, on the other hand, was a yellow-haired beauty stolen away by a Turkish sorcerer on a fire-breathing black horse. She too was restored to her mother at Eleusis, and ever since, according to local lore, "the fields have been fertile hereabouts."

IN 1801 a pair of British antiquarians found a colossal female statue buried up to the neck in a manure pile at Eleusis. The peasants revered this classical Demeter as an image of Saint Dhimitra, and they believed that it fertilized the steaming manure with which they in turn fertilized their fields. They sold the holy image with great reluctance, prophesying disaster to the Englishmen who were taking it away. Indeed the ship that brought Demeter, or Saint Dhimitra, to Britain went down off Beachy Head in the English Channel. The statue itself was recovered and set up in the Fitzwilliam Museum at Cambridge.

Next to the Virgin Mary, the patron saint of sailors is Nicholas, and every Greek ship has his image somewhere aboard. Nicholas has replaced pagan Poseidon, the sea god. Similarly, Saint Artemidos has supplanted ancient Artemis. Saint Dionysius stands for Dionysus, the pagan god of the vine. It is related that when this genial saint was still a child he plucked a pretty little plant that sprang from the ground before him. To keep the plant from withering he put it in the hollow leg bone of a bird, but as he was walking home the plant grew out around the bone, so he put the whole thing in the leg bone of a lion. Seeing it twine out of that bone too, he inserted it finally in the leg bone of an ass, and so planted it, bones and all, in his garden: "It sprang up quickly and to his delight bore the finest of grapes. Of these he at once made wine for the first time and gave it to men to drink. But now what wonders followed! When men drank of it, at first they sang like birds. When they drank deeper, they became strong as lions. When they drank deeper still, they resembled asses."

Nothing is easier than to smile at such "superstition." But it is not so easy to grasp the very real and ancient sense of nature from which it springs. Science tends to treat nature as fairly neutral material; human instinct, however, feels that living though invisible presences must inhabit the air, streams and mountains. This instinct has always been especially strong in Greece. Here nature still comes close to man. Here men find it difficult *not* to believe that glances dart upon thin air like transparent fish with good and evil intent, that nymphs are dancing and splashing in the waterfalls, that some islands are holy and that whole mountains can feel motherly sympathy for men.

As evidence, consider this ballad which dates from the Greek War of Independence. It concerns a raid made by Chief Androutsos and his Klepht tribesmen, mountaineers of Ghiona, against the Turkish garrison at the port of Itea on the plain below (the "Liakura" of the ballad is better known as Mount Parnassus):

And Ghiona calls to Liakura, and Liakura to Ghiona:
"Mountain, thou who art loftier and hast a higher vision,
What has become, tell me, of the Klephts of Androutsos?
Where do they roast their meat now? Where shoot they at the target?
What mountains do they now bedeck with Turkish heads?"

Shrine, Church and Temple

*"What shall I, mountain, say to thee? What,
   little mountain, shall I say?
The mangy plains rejoice in the youths;
They roast their meat on the plains, and shoot
   at the target;
The plains, too, do they bedeck with Turkish
   heads!"
Liakura, when she hears these words, is sorely
   grieved.
She looks to right and looks to left; she looks*

THE GODS OF THE PAST

The deities of ancient Greece were innumerable. Virtually every hill and spring was sacred to a divinity. Listed below are the major gods and their functions.

ZEUS, the supreme deity, was god of the sky and the weather, and ruled over all the other gods from his throne on Mount Olympus.

POSEIDON, brother of Zeus, ruled the sea and was also the Earthshaker, god of earthquakes.

HADES, the third brother, was lord of the underworld and king of the dead.

HESTIA, virgin sister of the three brothers, was goddess of the hearth and symbol of the home.

HERA, another sister, was the official wife of Zeus, queen of the heavens and protector of marriage.

ARES, the son of Zeus and Hera, was the god of war.

ATHENA, who sprang full-grown from the brow of Zeus, was goddess of wisdom and of civilized life.

APOLLO, son of Zeus and Leto, a goddess of earlier myths, was the much-loved god of the arts, of light and medicine.

APHRODITE, goddess of love and beauty, and beautiful herself, was born of the sea's foam.

HERMES, son of Zeus and a minor goddess, was his father's messenger and the protector of commerce.

ARTEMIS was the twin sister of Apollo and the chaste goddess of the hunt.

HEPHAESTUS, the ugly god of fire and handicrafts, was usually said to be the son of Zeus and Hera.

DEMETER, goddess of the earth, was a sister of Zeus.

DIONYSUS, a son of Zeus and a Theban princess, was god of the grape and thus of drinking.

When the Romans became influenced by Greek culture, they blended the Greek gods into their own pantheon. Thus the West sometimes knows Zeus as Jupiter or Jove, Poseidon as Neptune and Hades as Pluto. Hestia was renamed Vesta, Hera became Juno and Ares, Mars. Athena was the Roman Minerva, Aphrodite was Venus and Hermes was Mercury. Artemis became Diana, Hephaestus was called Vulcan, Demeter became Ceres and Dionysus, Bacchus.

---

*down on the port.
"Ah, Thou sickness-haunted plain, thou plain
   where lurks consumption,
With my own youths dost thou seek to deck
   thee?
Come, give me back my ornaments; give me
   back my youths,
Lest I melt all my snows and make thee waste
   as an ocean!"*

It has been stated that modern Greeks "are as pagan and as polytheistic in their hearts as ever were their ancestors." This seems exaggerated, yet scholars such as J. C. Lawson, Martin P. Nilsson, George A. Megas and A. B. Cook have amassed plenty of evidence to support the claim. For instance, animal sacrifice, which was basic to pagan religion, still is practiced in Greece. In rural areas a cock, a lamb or a young black bull wreathed in flowers and adorned with lighted candles is sacrificed to commemorate a feast or to pour life into any number of projects, from a journey to a barn-building. Every new bank or apartment house that goes up in Athens is consecrated by the blood of a slain cock.

Human sacrifice, that hydra-headed savagery, died hard in Greece. The earliest myths reek with it, and sometimes with cannibalism as well. The classic poets condemned it, yet the practice continued—in legendary Arcadia of all places—even perhaps into the Christian era. By the town of Arta in Epirus stands a high-arched bridge, many centuries old, of the utmost beauty. Greek balladeers still sing of its building. The foundations kept being swept away by the stream until the master mason understood what he must do. He summoned his beautiful bride to the bridge, saying, "Make ready slowly, dress slowly, come late in the afternoon. . . ." His bride came eagerly and soon, in all her finery. The master mason had her step down into the bridge foundations; then—

*One spread the mortar, one smoothed with
   the trowel,
the head artisan lifted and heaved a huge stone.*

Too late the dying bride recognized herself as a human sacrifice, to be killed in order that the bridge might live. Bitterly she framed a curse:

> 'As my heart quakes, may the bridge quake,
> 'as my hair falls, may those who pass fall!'

The masons pleaded with her, reminding her that her own brother might thus die on the bridge. And so she unsaid the first curse and pronounced another:

> 'May my heart be iron, may the bridge be iron,
> 'may my hair be iron and may those who pass be iron. . . .'

The bridge stood firm. To this day it remains a delight. And just as the death of the master mason's bride gave life to the bridge of Arta, so the death of paganism gave a special kind of life to Christianity in Greece. Many modern Greeks, as Professor Lawson notes, "are fully persuaded that God, Our Lady and the Saints go to and fro unseen above their heads, watch each man's actions and take part in his quarrels like the gods of Homer."

Asclepius, father of medicine, used to be invoked by the pagan sick. Suppliants spent the night, or sometimes days at a time, in the god's own sacred grounds, hoping to have a dream that could be interpreted favorably, thus effecting a cure. This manner of seeking health was called "incubation." Stone inscriptions describing 44 cures by incubation have been unearthed at Epidaurus, the greatest Asclepian shrine. Modern doctors tend to dismiss such cures as "autohypnosis," or in plain language, fooling oneself. But that oversimplifies the matter. Pagan priests were present to help the god do his work. Moreover the dreams experienced during incubation were often surprisingly medical. In one case a patient whose mouth was abscessed dreamed that "the god opened his mouth, held his jaws apart with a wedge, and cleansed the mouth. Thereupon he

THE FAITH OF THE PRESENT

Christianity long ago displaced the ancient gods of Greece. Today, the official state religion, to which virtually all citizens subscribe, is that of the Greek Church, a branch of Eastern Orthodoxy.

ORIGINS

Until the year 1054, when the Patriarch of Constantinople and the Roman Pope Leo IX excommunicated each other, the eastern and western branches of Christianity together constituted "One, Holy, Catholic and Apostolic Church." The 1054 split was both religious and political. The Roman church was often allied with the rulers of the West, the eastern church with the Byzantine emperors. Theologically, Eastern Orthodoxy objected to Rome's insertion of the phrase "and the Son" into the Nicene Creed, which both Christian branches used. The insertion made the creed express the belief that the Holy Ghost proceeds "from the Father and the Son." The Orthodox felt that the phrase suggested the possibility that there were two natures in God instead of the one traditionally accepted by theologians of both groups. In addition, the Orthodox objected to Rome's claim that it was the primary see of Christianity. The controversy might have been resolved, but after Roman Catholic Crusaders sacked Orthodox Constantinople in 1204, reconciliation became impossible.

ORGANIZATION

The Orthodox Church today is a loose federation which includes four independent, historic patriarchates—Constantinople, Jerusalem, Antioch and Alexandria—and 14 self-governing bodies located in various countries. Of these, only the Greek Church is an official state church. It is supported in part by government funds.

BELIEFS AND PRACTICES

While Orthodoxy refuses to accept the primacy of the Pope, and its rituals differ in detail from Rome's, Orthodox beliefs and practices closely parallel those of Roman Catholicism. To the layman the most obvious difference is that Orthodoxy admits married men to the priesthood. A married priest, however, cannot be promoted; in practice, therefore, celibate monks hold the ranking positions within the Orthodox hierarchy.

became well." A second suppliant dreamed that the god cut open his chest with a knife, took some leeches from the opening and gave them to him before stitching up the wound. "At daybreak he departed cured, with the leeches in his hand."

Christian saints carried on what others had begun. At Byzantium, for instance, the pagan heroes Castor and Polydeuces presided over a healing shrine until they were supplanted by a second pair of twin horsemen: Saints Cosmas and Damianos. The latter pair did just the same work at the same old stand, while sternly rebuking old-fashioned suppliants who confused them with their predecessors.

Health may be chiefly a matter of "good repair," or on the other hand it may require constant re-creation by forces far beyond the doctor's ken. Most Americans adopt the former view; the vast majority of Greeks accept the latter. Greece is very rich in "witches," that is, nonmedical doctors who specialize in faith cures and charms. Also, fear of the evil eye is widespread in Greece. Even a chic Athenian debutante may keep a blue bead sewed into her brassière as a protection against baleful glances from unknown sources. Sophisticated Greeks sometimes pooh-pooh the evil eye, however. They know that "any good witch can dispel its effects." And if witches fail, there is always the ancient remedy of incubation, still practiced at many Greek shrines.

THE little Aegean island of Tenos long ago held a sanctuary of "Poseidon the Healer." Today it has the richest church in Greece, built around an icon with far-famed healing powers. The icon is silver-plated and jewel-encrusted, with only the head of the Virgin and the Angel Gabriel left visible. It rests in a glass case crammed with diamond bracelets and similar offerings. The sick queue up for hours to kiss the glass, which an attendant priest keeps rubbing with a cloth dipped in cologne. The whole church gleams and blazes with rich presents from grateful pilgrims. Incubation produces eight to 10 apparently miraculous cures on Tenos every year.

Round about August 15 (the Virgin's feast day) and again toward March 25 (the day of the Annunciation), pilgrims by the thousands disembark at Tenos. All who can possibly squeeze into the church sleep there. The rest curl up in the squares, streets and alleys, just as close to the church walls as they can get. Dreaming blanket to blanket upon the pavement, they resemble in the darkest hours an immense and softly breathing flying carpet, winged with faith.

Puritanical missionaries from the West have always found Greece a stony pasture. The Reverend S. S. Wilson's *A Narrative of the Greek Mission,* published in 1839, put the problem candidly: "We had to combat with Christianity paganized. . . ." Once on a remote island Wilson found a "young warrior valiantly striking his lyre, and singing." He remonstrated with the man, explaining as best he could that "it is wicked" to sing nonreligious songs on Sunday, and suggesting a hymn fest instead. The warrior agreed to switch to hymns on one condition: "I shall expect your reverence to get up and dance." Wilson conscientiously records that, "As the young warrior made the last reply he smiled in good nature. I own I had not a reply: at least I find none in my notes."

On another occasion the minister was staying with the family of an Orthodox priest: "Before I rose from my mattress, I saw the priest get up, and was really amazed to see him wash his face and repeat his prayers at the same time; so as almost to fill his mouth with water and make it gurgle in his throat. Is this, one naturally asks, the spiritual, reverent, devout and prostrate devotion [one expects]?" Perhaps not, but the naturalness of the gurgling worshiper seems Greek indeed.

EVERY openhearted traveler in Greece finds more than merely physical refreshment at some stopping places. Often these pauses on the road occur where a marvelous view opens out, flooding the dusty mind with new volumes of clear light. Near at hand will be a tiny enclosed shrine containing a candle and an icon or perhaps just a colored picture of a sacred subject. Also, occasionally, a cool spring of fresh water and a great spreading tree with its roots in the spring. In conjunction with these elements, there often occurs, naturally enough, a little *taverna* which offers cheese, olives and a glass of wine. With luck there may be a Byzantine chapel besides, or even the remains of a pagan pedestal and inscription. The inscriptions that the ancient Greeks used to carve at such places give the clearest idea of them still. This one was written for a statue of the god Pan (and translated by J. W. Mackail):

"Here fling thyself down on the grassy meadow, O traveller . . . as thou listenest to the cicalas' tune, the stone-pine trembling in the wafts of west wind will lull thee, and the shepherd on the mountains piping at noon nigh the spring under a copse of leafy plane: so escaping the ardours of the autumnal dogstar thou wilt cross the height tomorrow; trust this good counsel that Pan gives thee."

HERE is another in a hauntingly archaic vein, written for a statue of Hermes by the girl epigrammatist Anyte of Tegea:

"I, Hermes, stand here by the windy orchard in the cross-ways nigh the grey sea-shore, giving rest on the way to wearied men; and the fountain wells forth cold stainless water."

Cold fresh springs are rare enough in Greece to be appreciated. The prettiest compliment that can be given a Greek peasant girl is to liken her not to wine or pearls or roses but to pure cold water. The compliment of course carries more than a hint of virginity as well as beauty. Like any hot-blooded but religious people the Greeks burn with ambiguous feelings about sex and love.

On Crete, the ancient home of the high-girdled Minoan mother goddess, a lovelorn girl sometimes "vows to the Virgin a silver girdle if she will lay her in her lover's arms." Meanwhile, over the horizon, her lover may be singing this island song:

> Our boat is endangered, Holy Virgin,
> In the deep waters.
> Help us to escape, Holy Virgin,
> And however many [lamps] you have,
> We will silver-plate them for you.
> I am not crying over the boat
>   or the money we'll lose,
> But over the young sailors, Holy Virgin,
> The hand-picked young sailors.

The Virgin's greatest Greek shrine had a long pagan history. In the year 316 B.C. a prince named Alexarchus of Macedonia founded Uranopolis—The City of Heaven—on a wild prong of Chalcidice. The town had its own coinage, with the sun for its emblem, and Alexarchus created a special language which, like Esperanto, he hoped to make universal. His utopian experiment did not last long, however; the city disappeared. Mount Athos, as the peninsula came to be called, reverted to obscurity. It was a high-backed, thick-forested, precipitous place, jutting about 40 miles into the northern Aegean Sea. The odor of its mountain herbs seemed to sanctify the air for miles about. Warlocks (male witches) would go there to seek out rare medicines, and an occasional huntsman would contest with the eagles for fat but wily hares.

Not long after the Crucifixion, as tradition relates, the Mother of God set sail for Cyprus with Saint John. A tempest carried them off course all the way to Athos. They anchored hard by a shrine of the sun god Apollo. But when Mary stepped ashore, Apollo's statue broke itself to bits. The Virgin refreshed herself on the shore, and before re-embarking blessed the "Holy Mountain," declaring it to be her garden—forbidden to all other women.

IN the Ninth Century a ship sailing by the wilderness tip of the peninsula seemed to take root in the sea and would not budge. A holy man aboard, whose name was Peter, declared that he had been called to remain on Athos. He swam ashore at present-day Karavostasi (The Bay of Standing Ships), and the sailors saw him climbing the grim ravine above. Then once again their ship sailed free. Over the years other hermits joined Peter on Athos. The first monastery on the Holy Mountain was founded in the 10th Century and was patronized by a major Byzantine emperor, Nicephorus Phocas. Ever since then, Athos has been the major Orthodox Christian contemplative center. Its saints and scholars alike have profoundly influenced the eastern half of Christendom for 1,000 years. Today, 32 monasteries and more than 600 hermitages nest like contemplative sea birds amongst the cliffs. No females of any kind (except hens and cats) are permitted to pass the crumbling wall that marks Athos' northern boundary. It is one of the few inhabited places upon earth where children's laughter can never be heard.

A MINORITY report on Athos was offered by eloquent Edward Lear, the landscape painter and composer of nonsense verse. He spent two months there in 1848, working well. Lear loved the scenery but declared that he would never go again "for any money, so gloomy, so shockingly unnatural, so lonely, so lying, so unatonably odious seems to me all the atmosphere of such monkery. That half of our species which it is natural to every man to cherish and love best, ignored, prohibited and abhorred [by] these muttering, miserable, mutton-hating, man-avoiding, misogynic, morose and merriment-marring, monotoning, many-mule-making, mocking, mournful, minched fish and marmalade masticating Monx! . . . As soon as Parliament meets, move that all [England's] distressed needlewomen be sent out at once to Mount Athos. Let the needlewomen be landed all at once, four thousand at least, on the . . . peninsula and make a rush for the nearest monastery; that subdued, all the rest will speedily follow."

Lear to the contrary, most laymen who have lived and worked on Athos report that it breathes an atmosphere of spiritual peace. The Holy Mountain remains home to more than 1,000 bearded, ragged, magnificently clear-eyed ascetics. There are few famous minds among them any more. Yet saints there may be. The self-containment and extreme gentleness of these monks command respect. They have withdrawn from sex and violence, from getting and spending, for reasons that seem quite sufficient to themselves. Some of them achieve a degree of charity not very often met with "in the world." This primary fact stands reflected in a brief harangue (overheard and written down by the English enthusiast Sidney Loch) given by an Athos muleteer to his beast: "Would you open those teeth of yours? Haven't I seen you nip a kind old monk? Such a kind old man. One of those who can't shake a bedbug out of his blanket without looking down to see if it's broken a leg!"

Passion Week, not Christmas, is the climax of the Greek holy year. Even the most worldly Greeks observe a rigorous fast in the days before Easter. Also they visit their family graves, saying that now the dead arise and inhabit the wild flowers of the April meadows. On Good Friday night, Jesus' bier is borne around the village or town by a candlelight procession of slow, solemn men and wailing women. On Saturday morning, spring lambs are slaughtered. In preparations for the Easter feast, the first egg thrown into the pot is for the Virgin herself, a sure protection against evil spirits.

TOWARD midnight on Saturday the whole community (except for widows and those in mourning) assembles in and around the church—all bringing unlighted candles. The schoolboys carry Roman candles and firecrackers besides. Only the earliest comers can see and hear the service in progress, until the priest, holding a lighted candle, interrupts it to come out of doors and mount a platform under the stars. He is chanting the Gospel story of the Resurrection. It is almost midnight. Now he sings, "Come ye, partake of the never-setting Light!" The clear flames dance and spread out, passing from candle to candle—like the sparking of a dark sea under an invisible rising sun —until every candle in the crowd is alight. Finally midnight comes, and the priest cries out, *"Christos Anesti!"* ("Christ Is Risen!"). The sea of candle flames lifts up.

Suddenly every church bell and ship's siren in the whole of Greece sounds forth. Now the candles dip and weave amid the first crackling blossoms of fireworks as the people embrace each other repeating and repeating, *"Christos Anesti!"* At this Easter moment, all Greece appears sanctified.

In token of reverence, a Macedonian village boy rises on tiptoe to kiss the hand of his parish priest, Father Panayotis Korkonzilas.

A Village Pastor's Manifold Concerns

Religion and ritual remain all-pervading forces in Greece. Some 90 per cent of the people are members of the Greek Orthodox faith, and virtually no enterprise is undertaken, no house raised, no crops sown without priestly blessing.

Particularly is this true in the small, remote villages. In one of these, Father Panayotis Korkonzilas fulfills the myriad spiritual and temporal duties of a rural pastor, as shown on the following pages in pictures by Richard Meek.

A COMMUNITY LEADER, the priest

AT HOME, Father Korkonzilas studies in his two-room apartment. Frequently university graduates, priests are often the best-educated men in the rural communities.

AT LUNCH, the priest talks with his wife, Anastasia (*left*). Greek Orthodox priests are permitted to marry before ordination. Their sons sometimes succeed them.

STROLLING WITH VILLAGERS, Father Korkonzilas gestures to the local president *(second from right)*, a farmer. Village presidents in Greece are elected, unpaid officials who act as combination mayors, counselors and chairmen of all community activities. No project is likely to be carried through without his and the priest's backing.

BRINGING SOLACE to the village's sick and disabled is a major pastoral task

HEAD BOWED, a bedridden village woman *(opposite)* prays with her priest. Women are the more devout of the villagers; men are infrequently seen at regular services.

LEARNING TO WALK, a paralytic injured in a fall is helped by the priest. A doctor from a medical clinic three miles away comes to visit the village twice a week.

VILLAGE CHILDREN, swinging school-bags, keep in close step with Father Korkonzilas. In many of the villages in northern Greece the priest also serves as the primary-school teacher.

SUNDAY SCHOOL is taught by the priest before a wall chart of the seasons. He uses the same small building which is employed during the rest of the week for regular school classes.

SUNDAY MASS is celebrated by the priest behind an altar screen in the village church. Father Korkonzilas spends much of his time trying to collect money for a larger church.

BREATHING FIRE, a paving machine,
made by the Barber-Greene Company
of Aurora, Illinois, heats asphalt for
one of the many new highways built
in Greece as part of an energetic program to modernize communications.

10

The Jagged Horizon

PREDICTIONS about the future of Greece
should be made with caution. Its record
in modern times is too checkered and moiled
with violence to cast much light ahead. All that
can be said for certain is that the Greeks will
never lose their identity as a race, their dignity
as individuals, their fierce love of freedom or
their desire to be rich.

Freedom and prosperity are worldwide goals.
Men differ bitterly at times on how to achieve
them in Greece. The present Greek economy is
gangling and uncertain. Politically the nation
faces external and internal threats. It occupies
an exposed position in the cold war. Civil strife

comprises a large part of its own tradition.
Moreover, as with many a tiny nation, it pitches
like a rowboat in political winds and economic
waves not of its own making.

For a time the United States gave this shaky
craft a tow. The U.S. life line is now being
cast off and Greece has set its own course
toward full membership in Europe's Common
Market. It will have a rough crossing, as everyone avers. Meanwhile America can view with
pride—but also with some regret—its own
past efforts for Greece. When the nation was
about to be delivered over to the Russian
dragon, America rescued it. Then, in the dark

succeeding years, U.S. taxpayers enabled Greek taxpayers to eat.

In all, the United States contributed nearly three billion dollars to Greece. The bulk of this money went for military aid, but much of it was in outright economic grants and technical assistance. The projects covered every conceivable area. United States missions demonstrated American farming techniques, trained the personnel for Greece's first agricultural extension service and established demonstration centers where farmers were shown how to pack farm produce. They set up schools in industrial management techniques, trained teachers for technical schools, and even helped to set up a radio communications network and a record-keeping system for the Greek police. Especially important for the long run was U.S. assistance in providing Greece with a passable road system and an electric power network.

Such largess was certainly not wasted. The value of the Greek agricultural output, for example, has risen by 40 per cent in the last few years. But the thoughts contributed were something else again. Whether for fear of rocking the boat or for reasons of misplaced modesty, the U.S. missions failed to bring American ideals to the fore in Greece.

TO this day Greek voters on the whole regard America as a kindly sort of Moloch, a brazen idol—rich, powerful, but empty. Basic American concepts of democratic process and of individual rights are not understood in Greece. Even those who profess democracy maintain that America's founding fathers added nothing to the tragic and essentially chaotic model of democracy which the ancient Greeks invented. Again, American principles of enlightened capitalism and labor-management cooperation are mistaken by the Greeks for luxuries, mere pie sharing and fine words. The fact that those same principles are integral parts of the American system seems incomprehensible to them.

In modern Greek politics and business alike, "influence" remains the all-important factor.

Everybody who is anybody has an angle, or a relative who does. Families form human pyramids to pluck what few plums there are on the tree. So loyalty wins trifles while initiative is penalized. The "good" jobs are almost as constraining as they are scarce. This makes for much polite despair in Athenian offices. But down around the corner, in the market place, is despair of a worse kind. There ragged housewives fiercely pinch at inviting fruit. Deals involving less than a nickel may become the subjects of intense dispute. A difference of a dollar can precipitate a brawl. Seen in proper perspective these dramas are not petty; they take place on the edge of an abyss of want.

BY comparison with the mean market towns and the glittering octopus that is Athens, the mountain and island villages of Greece seem heavenly. And they are so, except in one respect. The average villager's annual income amounts to less than $100. Fish, small game and home-grown vegetables enrich the village kitchens. Yet some degree of undernourishment remains the rule, not the exception, in remote parts of Greece. Following the worldwide pattern, more and more Greeks are migrating to the towns, especially to Athens. In Athens a man's sons can pick up some small change almost every day as bootblacks. His daughters may do a bit of embroidery to sell on street corners. And with luck he himself may get to carry cement for a few weeks on some construction project. All in all the average Athenian income is $350 a year.

Greece has pitifully few natural resources and very little power for industry. Manufactured products so far account for only a small proportion of the country's exports. Olive oil, wine, fruits, cotton and fine tobacco have for years made up the bulk of Greek trade. It has not been much to offer, since Europe happens to be rich in farm goods anyhow. One might expect tobacco to do well, but filter cigarettes have stunted the market for expensive and flavorsome tobaccos like the Greek. It would be most unfair to blame the nation's poverty upon its people. Greece always has been austere. Throughout history its important products have been art objects, poems and ideas.

If no titan of creativity has yet arisen in modern Greece, there is at least the cheerful ferment of experiment there, and the hope-charged atmosphere in which genius grows best. Greece has produced more than a dozen eloquent and delightful poets in the past 50 years. Best known in America is the late Nikos Kazantzakis, who dared write an epic sequel to Homer's *Odyssey*. Just now the rough and wild novels of young Vassilis Vassilikos are also being translated and published in the U.S. Greek painters of originality are few. But the humorous and tender canvases of a Cretan girl who signs herself "Athena" give great pleasure. On the whole, weavers—in a land where every girl learns to weave—have shown more skill and daring than painters. Elene Lorenzatos and Vienoula Kousathana have both deepened and broadened the weaving art.

IN music, the name to conjure with is Manos Hadjidakis, composer of "Never on Sunday." A rich heritage of Greek folk music underlies the sparkle of Hadjidakis' scores. Greek theater is lively, and occasionally lovely. Its most luminous figure at the moment is brilliant Melina Mercouri.

Engineering and architecture now, as in ancient times, draw many of the best Greek minds. Constantine A. Doxiadis, the Athens-based city planner, is undertaking bold developments in a dozen countries. His chief rival on the Athens scene is an American-trained engineer named Chris Sakellariades. From the Alps to the Caucasus Mountains, Sakellariades is responsible for a bewildering array of projects. Meanwhile the archeologist George Mylonas is bringing new light to bear on the achievements of classic architecture.

Intellectual and esthetic achievements do not in themselves produce wealth, however. They have of course little effect upon the No. 1 question in Greece—its economic life as a whole. In 1962 Greece committed itself to gradual absorption into the European Common Market. Can it hope to compete there?

Optimists point first to the extremely generous terms granted to Greece by the members of the Market—France, West Germany, Italy, Belgium, the Netherlands and Luxembourg, collectively known as the "Inner Six." Anxious to demonstrate that the Market could bring benefits to an underdeveloped nation, as it already had to their more industrialized economies, the Six permitted Greece a grace period of from 12 to 22 years to reduce its tariffs to the levels prevailing within the Market.

Moreover, Greece has made considerable economic strides in recent years. Emerging from the devastating civil war years, the country had rampant inflation and massive unemployment. Its economy was almost entirely dependent upon agriculture—in a setting in which 80 per cent of the land area is uncultivable. Its labor force was technically innocent, its capital scant. But under the strong-willed government of Premier Constantine Karamanlis, who took office in 1955, Greece managed to curb inflation. The government brought private funds out of hiding and into potential investment channels by increasing bank interest rates to 10 per cent. Moreover, Karamanlis set the country on a course toward industrialization, with some success. Since 1954, industrial output has increased at an average rate of 6.7 per cent a year, reaching a peak of 11 per cent in 1962.

MUCH of this increase has been achieved by attracting foreign investment. The availability of surplus Greek labor, the government's generous tax policies and the assurance of trading within the Common Market brought more than $100 million in foreign capital into Greece in 1962. Moreover, encouraged by a government mindful of the gap between relatively prosperous Athens and the grinding poverty of the rest of Greece, many of the new industries located in the provinces. Reynolds Metals of the U.S. began the construction of a $59 million aluminum plant near Delphi to utilize Greek bauxite, one of the few minerals which the country has in quantity. Dow Chemical opened a polystyrene plant at Lavrion, site of the gold and silver mines whose wealth financed the construction of the Parthenon. On the northern shore of the Peloponnesus, Pirelli Rubber of Italy was building a five-million-dollar tire plant; in Macedonia, Krupp of Germany was constructing a $2.5 million nickel and iron ore mill.

DESPITE these accomplishments, Greece's economic profile is far from flawless. Agriculture not only still accounts for one third of the national income but provides employment for more than half the population, and 25 per cent of the farmers can find work only part of the time. Most manufacturing remains concentrated in only a few industries. The overwhelming majority of Greek enterprises are still small, inefficient and family-owned. Out of the country's 109,000 firms only 9 per cent are partnerships and less than half of 1 per cent are stock companies.

Moreover, in joining the free-trading Common Market, the country faces stern readjustments in a cherished protectionist policy. Greek tariff walls, rising as high as 280 per cent, have created what one leading Greek economist calls "a xenophobic economy." John Pesmazoglu, the Athens banker who negotiated the country's entry into the Common Market, has remarked: "What our treaty amounts to is a test case for the Common Market and the free world. Greece must do in ten years what the highly industrialized nations of the West did in centuries."

This may seem impossible. But let us take a look at the positive side. Greece has a high literacy rate and excellent public health. A high percentage of Greek children at least get through grammar school. So Greece can supply strong, literate and eager manpower to the Common Market's migrant labor pool and to its own industries. Moreover the country has three hidden assets: an attraction for travelers, an international carrying trade and the generosity of its own sons abroad. Tourist expenditures in Greece now exceed $100 million annually. Greek sailors and shipowners bring home almost as much. Finally, family remittances from emigrants who have prospered in America and elsewhere add another $100 million. In the cramped perspective of Greek economics, such sums loom very large.

If foreign investors go on matching these hidden assets, Greece may come to hold its own within the Common Market. Improved business methods must be the first step, followed by a continued expansion of manufacturing. Eventually, Greece could become a sort of Southern California for Europe—a center of light industry. But such rosy dreams are still a long way from fulfillment. Meanwhile Greece keeps its own distinct glories, which austerity underlines.

Poverty, poetry and pain are kneaded into the daily bread of Greece. Whoever partakes of this bread understands Greece, and whoever subsists upon it knows the reality of a stark but lovely land. Now the Greeks themselves are coming more in contact with foreigners and foreign places. All too often in this wider world professional entertainers do the singing, visions are only for cameras, business sharpness passes for realism, and nature seems just something to exploit. So the question "What will become of Greece?" inevitably raises a still greater question in Greek minds: "What will become of the entire culture that was born in Greece?"

Whatever the future holds, it will not be kind to nations that stand alone; that much at least is clear. A fine contemporary poet, Odysseus Elytis, has precisely expressed the Hellenic temper in the world at large:

We will go together, and let them stone us
And let them say that we walk with our heads
*   in the clouds—*
Those who have never felt, my friend,
With what iron, what stones, what blood,
*   what fire,*
We build, dream and sing.

An elderly photographer awaits tourists at the Parthenon. Next page: Students play soccer in the ruins of the stadium at Epidaurus.

AMONG MONUMENTS *of their long and magnificent past, the Greeks . . .*

. . . strive boldly to prove that their forebears' ideal of the complete life, mixing

profound thought with decisive action, can be recaptured in the modern world

Appendix

HISTORICAL DATES

FOR FURTHER READING

CHAPTER 1: THE CLEAR LAND

Andrews, Kevin, *The Flight of Ikaros*. Houghton Mifflin, 1959.

Fermor, Patrick L., *Mani*. Harper & Brothers, 1958.

Gomme, A. W., *Greece*. Oxford University Press, 1946.

Hürlimann, Martin, and Rex Warner, *Eternal Greece*. Viking Press, 1953.

Lancaster, Osbert, *Classical Landscape with Figures*. John Murray, London, 1954.

Liddell, Robert, *Aegean Greece*. Jonathan Cape, London, 1954. *The Morea*. Jonathan Cape, London, 1958.

Miller, Helen H., *Greek Horizons*. Charles Scribner's Sons, 1961.

Payne, Robert, *The Splendor of Greece*. Harper & Brothers, 1960.

CHAPTER 2: ANCIENT HISTORY

Barr, Stringfellow, *The Will of Zeus*. J. B. Lippincott, 1961.

Bury, J. B., *A History of Greece*. Modern Library.

Finley, M. I., *The World of Odysseus*. Meridian Books, 1959.

Herodotus, *The Histories*. Aubrey de Selincourt, tr., Penguin Books.

Hutchinson, R. W., *Prehistoric Crete*. Penguin Books, 1962.

CHAPTER 3: A GOLDEN MOMENT

Bowra, Cecil Maurice, *The Greek Experience*. Mentor Book, 1962.

Burnet, John, *Early Greek Philosophy*. Meridian Books, 1959.

Farrington, Benjamin, *Greek Science*. Penguin Books, 1961.

Kitto, H.D.F., *The Greeks*. Penguin Books, 1962.

Rodocanachi, C. P., *Athens and the Greek Miracle*. Routledge and Kegan Paul, London, 1948.

Thucydides, *Complete Writings*. Richard Crawley, tr., Modern Library, 1951.

Zimmern, Alfred E., *The Greek Commonwealth*. Modern Library.

CHAPTER 4: DECLINE AND SUBJUGATION

Artz, Frederick B., *The Mind of the Middle Ages*. Alfred A. Knopf, 1954.

Baynes, N. H., and H. St. L. B. Moss, eds., *Byzantium*. Oxford University Press, 1961.

Botsford, George Willis, and C. A. Robinson, *Hellenic History*. Macmillan, 1956.

Cambridge Medieval History, The, Vol. IV. Macmillan, 1927.

Gibbon, Edward, *Christianity and the Decline of Rome* (Vol. I of *The Decline and Fall of the Roman Empire*). Washington Square Press, 1962.

Tarn, W. W., *Hellenistic Civilization*. Meridian Books, 1961.

Toynbee, Arnold J., *Hellenism*. Oxford University Press, 1959.

Vasiliev, Alexander A., *History of the Byzantine Empire*, 2 vols. University of Wisconsin Press, 1960.

CHAPTER 5: A NEW NATION

Byford-Jones, W., *Greek Trilogy*. Hutchinson, London, 1945.

Forster, Edward S., *A Short History of Modern Greece, 1821-1956*. Frederick A. Praeger, 1958.

Howe, Samuel G., *Greek Revolution*. White, Gallaher & White, 1828.

Kousoulas, Dimitrios G., *The Price of Freedom: Greece in World Affairs, 1939-1953*. Syracuse University Press, 1953.

Larrabee, Stephen, *Hellas Observed*. New York University Press, 1957.

Leeper, Reginald, *When Greek Meets Greek*. Chatto & Windus, London, 1950.

McNeill, William Hardy, *The Greek Dilemma*. J. B. Lippincott, 1947.

Pallis, Alexander A., *Greece's Anatolian Adventure—and After*. Methuen, London, 1937.

Smothers, Frank, and others, *Report on the Greeks*. Twentieth Century Fund, 1948.

Sweet-Escott, Bickham, *Greece: A Political and Economic Survey, 1939-1953*. Royal Institute of International Affairs, London, 1954.

Woodhouse, C. M., *Apple of Discord*. Hutchinson, London, 1948.

Xydis, Stephen G., *Greece and the Great Powers: 1944-1947*. Institute for Balkan Studies, Thessaloniki, Greece, 1963.

CHAPTER 6: THE ARTS

Diehl, Charles, *Byzantium, Greatness and Decline*. Rutgers University Press, 1957.

Grabar, André, *Byzantine Painting*. Skira, Geneva, 1953.

Lawrence, Arnold W., *Greek Architecture*. Penguin Books, 1957.

Lullies, Reinhard, *Greek Sculpture*. Harry N. Abrams, 1957.

Richter, Gisela M. A., *A Handbook of Greek Art*. Oxford University Press, 1960.

Robertson, Martin, *Greek Painting*. Skira, Geneva, 1959.

Seltman, Charles, *Approach to Greek Art*. E. P. Dutton, 1960.

Talbot Rice, David, *Byzantine Art*. Oxford University Press, 1935.

CHAPTER 7: LITERATURE, PHILOSOPHY

Aristophanes, *Complete Plays*. Moses Hadas, ed., Bantam Books, 1962.

Aristotle, *Basic Works*. Richard McKeon, ed., Random House, 1941.

Auden, W. H., ed., *The Portable Greek Reader*. Viking Press, 1955.

Grene, David, and Richmond Lattimore, eds., *The Complete Greek Tragedies*, 4 vols. University of Chicago Press, 1960.

Hadas, Moses, *A History of Greek Literature*. Columbia University Press, 1950.

Higham, T. F., and C. M. Bowra, eds., *Oxford Book of Greek Verse in Translation*. Oxford University Press, 1938.

Highet, Gilbert, *The Classical Tradition*. Galaxy Book, 1957.

Homer, *The Iliad*. Richmond Lattimore, tr., University of Chicago Press, 1962. *The Odyssey*. E. V. Rieu, tr., Penguin Books.

Plato, *The Portable Plato*. Scott Buchanan, ed., Viking Press, 1948.

CHAPTER 8: A GUEST LIST

Hamilton, Edith, *The Greek Way to Western Civilization*. Mentor Book, 1961.

Huxley, Michael, ed., *The Root of Europe*. Oxford University Press, 1953.

Livingstone, Richard, ed., *The Legacy of Greece*. Oxford University Press, 1921.

MacKendrick, Paul, *The Greek Stones Speak*. St. Martin's Press, 1962.

Miller, Henry, *The Colossus of Maroussi*. New Directions, 1958.

Palmer, Leonard R., *Mycenaeans and Minoans*. Alfred A. Knopf, 1962.

CHAPTER 9: RELIGION

Bulfinch, Thomas, *The Age of Fable*. Mentor Book, 1962.

Cornford, F. M., *From Religion to Philosophy*. Harper & Brothers, 1957.

Frazer, James George, *The Golden Bough*. Macmillan, 1960.

Graves, Robert, *The Greek Myths*. Braziller, 1957.

Kerényi, Károly, *The Heroes of the Greeks*. Grove Press, 1960.

Nilsson, Martin P., *Greek Folk Religion*. Harper Torchbooks, 1961.

CHAPTER 10: GREECE TODAY

Charioteer, The. Parnassos Greek Cultural Society of New York, Vol. 1, Nos. 1, 2, 3, 4.

Dalven, Rae, ed., *Modern Greek Poetry*. Gaer Associates, 1949.

Dawkins, R. M., ed., *Modern Greek Folktales*. Oxford University Press, 1953.

Keeley, Edmund, and Philip Sherrard, eds., *Six Poets of Modern Greece*. Alfred A. Knopf, 1961.

McNeill, William Hardy, *Greece: American Aid in Action, 1947-1956*. Twentieth Century Fund, 1957.

Munkman, C. A., *American Aid to Greece*. Frederick A. Praeger, 1958.

"Perspective of Greece." An *Atlantic* supplement. June 1955.

Sanders, Irwin, *The Rainbow in the Rock*. Harvard University Press, 1962.

Stanford, W. B., *The Ulysses Theme*. Basil Blackwell & Mott, Oxford, 1955.

Trypanis, C. A., ed., *Medieval and Modern Greek Poetry: An Anthology*. Oxford University Press, 1951.

FAMOUS GREEK CULTURAL FIGURES AND THEIR PRINCIPAL WORKS

ART AND ARCHITECTURE

Execias	6th Century B.C.	Vase painting: black-figured *Ajax and Achilles Playing Draughts, Dionysus Sailing Over the Sea*
Duris	fl. c.510-465	Vase painting: red-figured *Eos and Memnon;* two women putting away clothes
Euphronius	6th-5th Centuries	Vase painting: red-figured *Heracles Wrestling with Antaeus*
Apollodorus	5th Century	Painting: experimented with shading; no extant works
Hippodamus	5th Century	Architecture: associated with the rectangular gridiron system in town planning
Myron	fl. c.480-c.445	Sculpture: bronze figures, known from copies; *Discobolus (Discus Thrower), Athena and Marsyas*
Agatharcus	fl. c.468-c.430	Painting: scene painter for Aeschylus; first to use perspective on a large scale
Ictinus	fl. after 450	Architecture: one of the Parthenon architects
Callicrates	fl. after 450	Architecture: associated with Ictinus in the building of the Parthenon
Phidias	c. 490-?	Sculpture: known from descriptions; ivory and gold *Athena Parthenos* and bronze *Athena Promachos* for the Acropolis; ivory and gold *Zeus* for Olympia; extant marble sculptures of the Parthenon were designed, if not executed, by him
Polygnotus	fl. 475-c.447	Painting: large murals in the Cnidian Lesche at Delphi and the Stoa Poikile in Athens, known from descriptions
Polycletus	fl. c.450-c.405	Sculpture: bronze statues of Olympic victors; *Doryphoros* and *Diadumenos,* known from copies
Zeuxis	fl. c.425	Painting: noted for realism; added highlights to shading; no extant works
Parrhasius	fl. c.400	Painting: also noted for realism; no extant works
Apelles	4th Century	Painting: known from descriptions; *Aphrodite* rising from the sea and wringing water from her hair; portraits of Philip and Alexander
Scopas	4th Century	Sculpture: associated with style reflecting pain or grief
Praxiteles	c.364-?	Sculpture: extant marble *Hermes* with infant Dionysus on his arm; reputed in antiquity: *Aphrodite of Cnidus, Eros, Satyr*
Lysippus	fl. c.340-c.300	Sculpture: famous for his slender forms and precision of detail; bronze *Apoxyomenos* (known from a marble copy)
Apollonius of Athens	fl. c.50	Sculpture: marble *Torso Belvedere*
Agesander	1st Century A.D.	Sculpture: marble *Laocoön* group, done with sculptors Polydorus and Athenodorus
Anthemius	fl. c.530	Architecture: Hagia Sophia church at Constantinople, with Isidorus
Anonymous	Byzantine period	Outstanding contributions, particularly icon paintings, mosaics, frescoes and book illuminations
Parthenis, Constantine	1879-	Painting: *The Annunciation, Orpheus and Eurydice, The Apotheosis of Athanasios Diakos*
Tombros, Michael	1889-	Sculpture: *Woman Swimmer, Two Friends, Ephebos;* works in bronze, marble and plaster
Gounaro, George	1890-	Painting: creates fantasy world with experiments of light
Kondoglou, Photis	1895-	Painting: iconography; also applies Byzantine principles to secular art
Ghika (Nicos Hadzikyriakos)	1906-	Painting: landscapes, particularly of the island of Hydra; illustrations of the *Odyssey*
Kapralos, Chrestos	1909-	Sculpture: *Christophoros, Vlachos, The Drunkard;* works mostly in marble
Tsarouhis, Yiannis	1910-	Painting: soldiers and sailors of World War II, cafe life; also stage and costume design

LITERATURE

Homer	8th Century? B.C.	Epic poetry: *Iliad* and *Odyssey,* earliest known works of Greek literature
Hesiod	7th Century?	Poetry: after Homer, the most famous of Greek epic poets; *Works and Days, Theogony*
Alcman	c.654-c.611	Lyric poetry: songs of Spartan feasts and festivals
Solon	c.640-c.560	Famous as a statesman, he expressed his moral, political and social views in poetry
Sappho	c.612-?	Lyric poetry: love poems; solo hymns to Aphrodite and the Muses
Aesop	6th Century?	Fables: credited with originating many animal anecdotes with moral conclusions
Simonides of Ceos	c.556-c.468	Poetry: odes and elegies; an epigram on the Spartans who fell at Thermopylae
Thespis	fl. c.534	Drama: semilegendary poet, actor and dramatist said to have introduced an actor into performances of choral groups
Aeschylus	c.525-c.456	Drama: earliest of great Attic tragedians, seven of whose works survive: *Oresteia* trilogy, *Suppliants, Persians, Seven Against Thebes, Prometheus Bound;* introduced second actor into performances
Pindar	c.518-c.438	Poetry: choral odes honoring the victors at the Olympic and other games
Sophocles	c.496-c.406	Drama: second of Attic tragedians; introduced third actor; surviving from some 120 plays: *Antigone, Oedipus Rex, Electra, Ajax, Trachiniae, Philoctetes, Oedipus at Colonus*
Euripides	c.485-c.406	Drama: third Attic tragedian, whose interest lay in human ideas and emotions; among his 19 extant works: *Medea, Hippolytus, Orestes, Andromache, Electra*
Herodotus	c.485-?	History and travel: *Persian Wars,* in which he attempted to document his historical judgments
Thucydides	c.460-c.400	History: *Peloponnesian War,* including Pericles' eloquent funeral oration
Aristophanes	c.455-c.385	Drama: chief representative of the Old Comedy of sharp satire; his works include: *Frogs, Knights, Clouds, Birds, Lysistrata*
Isocrates	c.436-c.338	Oratory and political writings: *Panegyricus,* devoted to the cause of unity for Greece
Xenophon	c.430-c.354	History: recollections of his association with Socrates; *Anabasis,* his experiences in Persia
Demosthenes	c.384-c.322	Oratory: *Philippics,* a series of speeches warning Athenians against Philip of Macedonia
Menander	c.342-c.291	Drama: New Comedy style; only fragments are extant: *The Arbitration, The Rape of the Ringlets, Samia*
Callimachus	c.305-c.240	Poetry and criticism: Alexandrian scholar, known especially for his epigrams
Strabo	c.48 B.C.-c.19 A.D.	Geography: *Geography,* in 17 books, of the chief countries of the Roman world

154

Plutarch	c.46-c.127 A.D.	Biography and philosophy: *Parallel Lives*, comparative biographies of Greek and Roman statesmen and soldiers
Pausanias	fl. c.150	History: wrote the first guidebook, *Description of Greece*
Clement of Alexandria (Titus Flavius Clemens)	c.150-c.215	Theology: in *Hortatory Address to the Greeks*, he extolled Christianity over paganism
Origen (Origenes Adamantius)	c.185-c.254	Theology: *Hexapla*, a prodigious critical edition of the Old Testament
Longus	3rd Century?	Novel: *Daphnis and Chloe*, a pastoral romance
Eusebius of Caesarea	c.260-c.340	History and biography: Greek, Roman and church histories; a biography of Constantine
Procopius	c.490-c.565	History: wrote officially on the wars of Justinian and unofficially on the scandals of the court
Romanus Melodus	fl. c.520	Poetry: religious hymns utilizing Biblical stories
Paul the Silentiary	fl. c.540	Poetry: a poem in Homeric hexameters describing the architectural wonders of Hagia Sophia church
Photius, Patriarch of Constantinople	820-891	Theology, history, etc.: *Biblioteca*, a vast critical analysis of historical prose works
Constantine Porphyrogenetus, Emperor	905-959	History: *On the Administration of the Empire; On the Ceremonies of the Byzantine Court*
Eustathius, Archbishop of Thessalonica	?-c.1194	Commentaries on classical authors: reform pamphlets; a history of the Norman conquest of Thessalonica
Kalvos, Andreas	1792-1867	Poetry: *Odes*
Solomos, Dionysios	1798-1857	Poetry: *Hymn to Liberty, The Free Besieged*, first to use the demotic idiom
Papadiamandis, Alexandros	1851-1911	Short stories: *Phonissa (Murderess), The Yearly Victim*
Palamas, Kostis	1859-1943	Poetry: *The Twelve Words of the Gypsy;* also plays, short stories, essays, criticism
Kavafis, Constantine	1863-1933	Poetry: *Waiting for the Barbarians, The Walls, God Forsaking Anthony*
Karkavitsas, Andreas	1866-1923	Novels: *Tales of the Forecastle, The Beggar*
Sikelianos, Angelos	1880-1951	Poetry: *The Visionary, Mother of God, The Easter of the Greeks*
Kazantzakis, Nikos	1885-1957	Novels: *Zorba, the Greek, The Greek Passion;* poetry: *The Odyssey: A Modern Sequel*
Myrivilis, Stratis	1892-	Novels: *Life in the Tomb, The School Mistress with the Golden Eyes, The Mermaid Madonna*
Seferis, George	1900-	Poetry: *The King of Asine and Other Poems*
Venezis, Elias	1904-	Novels: *Aeolia, Number 31328;* play: *Block C*
Elytis, Odysseus	1911-	Poetry: *Orientations, Sun, the First, Six and One Remorses of Conscience for the Sky*

PHILOSOPHY AND SCIENCE

Thales Anaximander Xenophanes Anaximenes	7th-6th Centuries B.C.	Pre-Socratic Ionian philosophers and "physicists," concerned with finding unity in the universe
Pythagoras	fl. c.530	Combined mysticism and mathematics
Parmenides	c.510-?	Founder of the Eleatic school of philosophy
Heraclitus	fl. c.500	Propounded a doctrine of tensions and flux
Anaxagoras	c.500-c.428	Introduced the investigation of natural science; explained solar eclipses
Empedocles	c.493-c.433	Wrote *On Nature* and *Purifications;* discovered that air is a substance rather than empty space
Protagoras	c.485-?	Sophist whose dictum was "man is the measure of all things"
Socrates	c.469-c.399	Wrote nothing himself but was interpreted by Plato and others, and greatly influenced later philosophical thought
Hippocrates	c.460-?	Founded a school of medicine at Cos; his name survives in the Hippocratic Oath, although nothing remains of his actual works
Leucippus Democritus	5th Century	Developed the theory of atoms
Antisthenes	c.455-c.360	Considered the founder of the Cynic school of philosophy
Plato	c.429-c.347	His philosophical thought is presented in the form of dialogues in a prose style often raised to poetical heights; among his works: *Apology* (Socrates' defense at his trial), *Symposium, Republic, Phaedo, Phaedrus, Timaeus, Laws*
Aristotle Theophrastus Aristoxenus	4th Century	Teachers in the Peripatetic school in Athens, founded by Aristotle, who organized research on a vast scale; they contributed important works to many fields of knowledge
Epicurus	c.342-c.271	Founded the Epicurean school of philosophy; held that the highest good is pleasure (or absence of pain), to be found in intellectual pursuits rather than frivolity or indulgence
Zeno	c.335-c.263	Founded the Stoic school of philosophy; taught that the only good is virtue
Aristarchus of Samos	c.310-c.230	Alexandrian scholar; theorized that the earth revolved around a larger, stationary sun
Euclid	fl. c.300	Wrote *Elements*, used as a geometry textbook until the 20th Century
Herophilus	fl. c.300	Wrote *On Anatomy, Of the Eyes*
Archimedes	c.287-c.212	Set down the laws of equilibrium; inventor in physics and mechanics
Eratosthenes	c.275-c.194	Calculated, almost accurately, the earth's circumference; tried to fix dates in history
Hipparchus	c.190-c.125	Discovered and measured the precession of the equinoxes; invented trigonometry; calculated the lunar month to within one second
Ptolemy (Claudius Ptolemaeus)	fl. c.150 A.D.	Wrote *Almagest (The Mathematical Collection in Thirteen Books)*
Galen	c.129-c.199	Wrote *Anatomical Exercises*

Credits

The sources for the illustrations in this book are shown below: Credits for pictures from left to right are separated by commas, top to bottom by dashes.

Cover: Dmitri Kessel

8, 9—Richard Meek

14 through 19—Richard Meek

20, 21—Paul Mitarachi except center; Joseph Nettis

22, 23—Richard Meek except top left; Peter Throckmorton from Nancy Palmer Agency

24—Richard Meek

28—Map by Bill Dove

32—Richard Meek

33—James Burke

34, 35—Joseph Nettis except right; Richard Meek

36, 37, 38—Richard Meek

40—From *Zeus* by A. B. Cook, Cambridge University Press

43—Courtesy of the American School of Classical Studies at Athens, rendering by Bill Dove

45—James Burke

46, 47, 48—Richard Meek

49—Louise Dahl-Wolfe

50, 51—Culver Pictures

52—The Bettmann Archive

54, 55—Drawings by Burt Silverman

57—Richard Meek

58, 59—Joseph Nettis

60, 61—Dmitri Kessel

62—Richard Meek

66—Chart by Bill Dove

70—Dmitri Kessel

71—Dmitri Kessel—David Douglas Duncan, Radio Times Hulton Picture Library

72, 73—James Burke except right; Richard Meek

74, 75—Richard Meek

76, 77—Max Hirmer courtesy Harry N. Abrams, Inc.

81—From *The New Century Classical Handbook*, edited by Catherine B. Avery, copyright © 1962 by Appleton Century-Crofts, Inc., reproduced by permission of Appleton Century-Crofts

83—National Museum of Athens

84, 85—Max Hirmer courtesy Harry N. Abrams, Inc.

86, 87—Courtesy The Byzantine Institute of America

88—Max Hirmer courtesy Harry N. Abrams, Inc.

89—The Metropolitan Museum of Art Rogers Fund, 1951, The Metropolitan Museum of Art gift of Colonel and Mrs. Lewis Landes, 1958—The Metropolitan Museum of Art Rogers Fund, 1906, The Metropolitan Museum of Art Rogers Fund, 1907

90, 91—Fred Kenett

92, 93—David Lees

94, 95—Dimitrios Harissiadis

103 through 107—Richard Meek

108—Richard Meek except top right; Edward Quinn

109—Burt Glinn from Magnum

110—Edward Steichen

116—Courtesy University of Cincinnati, Photo by Alison Frantz—Drawing by Matt Greene

118 through 128—Richard Meek

137 through 144—Richard Meek

149, 150, 151—Richard Meek

ACKNOWLEDGMENTS

The editors of this book are indebted to Dr. Stephen G. Xydis, a specialist in modern Greek affairs, who served as general consultant on the text. The editors are also indebted to Moses Hadas, Jay Professor of Greek at Columbia University, and Ihor Ševčenko, Professor of Byzantine History, Columbia University, both of whom read and commented on portions of the text. Valuable assistance was also rendered by Homer A. Thompson, Professor of Classical Archaeology, the Institute for Advanced Study, Princeton, New Jersey, and Field Director, Agora Excavation, American School of Classical Studies at Athens; by Lucy Shoe, editor of *Hesperia, Journal of the American School of Classical Studies at Athens;* by James A. Coulter, Instructor of Greek and Latin, Columbia University; and by Brian F. Cook, Assistant Curator of Greek and Roman Art, The Metropolitan Museum of Art.

The editors wish also to express their gratitude for the research and advice given by Andonis Decavalles, Assistant Professor of English at Fairleigh Dickinson University and coeditor of *The Charioteer*, and by Mr. and Mrs. Peter Chaitin and Rita Langford.

Index

This symbol in front of a page number indicates a photograph or painting of the subject mentioned.

158

Production staff for Time Incorporated
Arthur R. Murphy Jr. (Vice President and Director of Production)
Robert E. Foy, James P. Menton and Caroline Ferri
Text photocomposed under the direction of
Albert J. Dunn and Arthur J. Dunn

✕

Printed by R. R. Donnelley & Sons Company, Crawfordsville, Indiana,
and The Safran Printing Company, Detroit, Michigan
Bound by R. R. Donnelley & Sons Company, Crawfordsville, Indiana
Paper by The Mead Corporation, Dayton, Ohio

Date Due